T0307890

The Authenticity of the Gospels

THE AUTHENTICITY OF THE GOSPELS

Peter LP Simpson

ELM HILL

A Division of
HarperCollins Christian Publishing

www.elmhillbooks.com

The Authenticity of the Gospels

Published in Nashville, Tennessee, by Elm Hill, an imprint of Thomas Nelson. Elm Hill and Thomas Nelson are registered trademarks of HarperCollins Christian Publishing, Inc.

Elm Hill titles may be purchased in bulk for educational, business, fund-raising, or sales promotional use. For information, please e-mail SpecialMarkets@ ThomasNelson.com.

Library of Congress Cataloging-in-Publication Data

Library of Congress Control Number: 2019931603

ISBN 978-1-400325429 (Paperback)
ISBN 978-1-400325436 (Hardbound)
ISBN 978-1-400325443 (eBook)

Acknowledgement

My sincere thanks to Rev. Randy Soto for guiding me in the study of the Gospels and in the Historical Critical Method as applied to them

And to both him and Dr. Marianne Siegmund for encouraging me to publish these results of my research and reflections

TABLE OF CONTENTS

For we did not follow cleverly devised myths when we made known to you the power and coming of our Lord Jesus Christ, but we had been eyewitnesses of his majesty.
(2 Peter 1.16)

We declare to you what was from the beginning, what we have heard, what we have seen with our eyes, what we have looked at and touched with our hands, concerning the word of life...
(1 John 1.1)

INTRODUCTION

The aim of this book is to confirm the long-standing historical tradition that the Gospels are the authentic documents of their traditional authors and accurately record, after the manner of eye witness memoirs, actual events, deeds, and sayings in the earthly life of Our Lord.

The book, however, does not so much confirm this claim by direct examination of the history within the Gospels (which would be a large project and has been done by others[1]) but to do so rather by refuting the view, made popular by those who claim to be using the so-called historical critical method or to be speaking in the name of the scientific method, that the authors of the Gospels are *not* those traditionally identified (the Apostles Matthew and John, and Mark and Luke the followers of the Apostles Peter and Paul).[2] The main reason for such a procedure is that

---

[1] Older authors are perhaps better here than modern ones, and certainly deserve to be better remembered, in particular Nathaniel Lardner, *The Credibility of the Gospel History; or, the facts occasionally mention'd in the New Testament; confirmed by passages of ancient authors who were contemporary with Our Saviour or His apostles, or lived near their time.* (London: J. Chandler, 1727); and Thomas. H. Horne *A Summary of the Evidence for the Genuineness, Authenticity etc. of the Holy Scriptures* (London: Longman, Green, and Roberts, 1860). Both these books are available through Google books. See also John Duns Scotus, *Ordinatio*, Prologue, Part Two, in Ioannis Duns Scoti. *Opera omnia.* Vol. 1, ed. C. Balić, et al. (Vatican City: Typis Polyglottis Vaticanis, 1950).

[2] Those who hold this view are legion, but it seems to arise first from people like Reimarus, Schleiermacher, and Strauss in the 18th and 19th Centuries, and then to get refined and developed by innumerable others, as Harnack, Streeter, Loisy, Wrede, Wellhausen, Schweitzer, Dibelius, Bultmann, Lightfoot. There is a summary in Bernard Orchard, Edmund Sutcliffe, et al. *A Catholic Commentary on Holy Scripture*

the wide acceptance of this method and of its presuppositions by most Biblical scholars (whether Catholic, Protestant, or unaligned) stands in the way of a fair assessment of the historicity of the Gospels. For the method calls into doubt, or rather denies, that the Gospels are authentic documents of their supposed authors.

Authenticity of historical records is integral to history as such, since it is only because we have authentic records that we can rely on them for learning the truth about history. If a supposed authentic record turns out not to be authentic, or not to have the author and date it claims to have, its historical value is thrown into doubt. The doubt can only be removed by showing that the true author and date (if they can be found) give the record the necessary historical reliability.

The historical critical method does not remove this doubt but, if anything, confirms it. If the historicity of the Gospels is to be maintained, the method must be countered, for if it is not countered the Gospels cannot be held to be authentic historical records. Countering the method is, surprisingly, easier to do than the wide acceptance of the method would lead one to suppose. A serious critical examination, from the point of view of both reason and fact, shows that the method, as typically deployed, lacks adequate foundation. Indeed, to the extent that the method is well founded, it proves the opposite of what it is taken to prove.

The historical critical method, if truth be told, is not historical in how it approaches the Gospel texts or in how it treats the historical evidence about their dating and authorship. It is not critical, or not sufficiently critical, in how it reads the texts, wherein it also displays a certain

---

(London: Thomas Nelson & Sons, 1953) §§604a-609e, pp.752-759. A fuller summary can be found in William Farmer, *The Synoptic Problem. A Critical Analysis* (New York: Macmillan, 1964), and in Werner Kümmel, *Introduction to the New Testament*. Trans. A.J. Mattill (London: SCM Press, 1966). The scholars mentioned are mainly non-Catholics but a number of Catholic scholars share similar views, as notably John P. Meier, *A Marginal Jew. Rethinking the Historical Jesus*. 5 vols. (London: Doubleday, and Yale University Press, 1991-2016). Some scholars, of course, defend the traditional view about the authorship of the Gospels, as Farmer and Orchard above cited, and Orchard and Harold Riley together in *The Order of the Synoptics. Why Three Synoptic Gospels?* (Macon Ga.: Mercer University Press, 1987). These scholars come from both the Protestant and Catholic traditions.

woodenness of literary analysis. Elements of the method have a place in Gospel reading and research, but historical and literary sense as well as the teachings of great theologians of the past require them to be used in ways very different from those standardly adopted.

This book is therefore both philosophical and historical. It is philosophical because the method and principles of the science of history, as of any science, are matters for philosophical examination and critique. Only if the science of history is properly understood can the question of the historicity of the Gospels, or of any text whether ancient or modern, be properly broached. The book is historical because the authenticity of any supposed historical document, which is central to the question of the reliability of the document and of the truth of what it says, must be assessed by reference to the historical evidence. Such evidence is properly extrinsic to the literary features of a text and cannot be judged by the methods of literary criticism alone, or at all in many cases.

The book divides into the following parts. In the first chapter, which will serve also as a more focused introduction, the existential nature of all history, whether as the human deeds themselves or also the human recording of those deeds, will be stated and defended. The historical critical method is not unaware of this existentiality (it regularly notes it in terms of what it calls the *Sitz im Leben*, or the "life situation," of the Gospels), but fails to follow it properly.

In the second chapter the larger question of the method of history as such will be examined. The chapter will begin with discussion of the method followed by one of the more notable and more recent of writers on the Gospels and their history, namely John P. Meier in his *A Marginal Jew: Rethinking the Historical Jesus*. Meier's method, which is an application of the historical critical method, will be found not to be a method of history. The chapter will proceed to an examination of the historical critical method proper: its parts, its presuppositions, its approach to history, its approach to literary analysis. All these elements of the method as the method is typically practiced will be critically examined and found to be wanting in philosophical, historical, and literary sense.

In the third chapter there will be discussion of the very limited role that literary analysis can properly play in settling historical questions, and particular instances of analysis of Gospel passages will be examined to prove the need not to transgress this limited role.

In the fourth chapter the historical evidence for the authenticity and authorship of the Gospels will be discussed. The dismissive treatment of this evidence by contemporary practitioners of the historical critical method will be examined and shown to be without philosophical warrant. The historical evidence will be reviewed in summary form and the conclusion that it should be accepted by any sound use of the historical method will be argued for against the doubts and denials and rejections of contemporary scholars.

The fifth chapter, the final chapter, will reconsider the historical critical method in the light of what has been said in earlier chapters. It will be argued that the method has a proper use and that, if it this proper use is followed, very fruitful results can be achieved that combine and neatly harmonize all the relevant evidence (philosophical, historical, literary), instead of prioritizing one of these over another. A concrete example is given from the work of Orchard and Riley (a Catholic and an Anglican respectively working together), which, even if not correct in all its details, shows how easy it is to use the historical critical method to give a compelling defense of the authenticity and historicity of the Gospels.[3]

Worth stressing here is that the opinions examined in what follows, as well as the assessment of them in the light of both facts and reason, are ecumenical in character. Scholars on both sides of the question of authenticity come from the full spectrum of Christian allegiance or non--allegiance: Catholic, Protestant, committed, opposed, agnostic, atheist. Arguments for authenticity, as well as arguments against, are espoused by representatives of all or most Christian traditions. For whatever other differences in doctrine or practice exist between them, all the traditions are affected by the debate and all have found themselves internally divided

---

[3] Orchard and Riley *The Order of the Synoptics. Why Three Synoptic Gospels?*

over it. To come down on one side of the debate, as this book does, is not to be aligned with Protestants more than with Catholics, with Catholics more than with Protestants, or with believers more than non-believers. Assertion and especially denial of Gospel authenticity are, so to say, equal opportunity employers.[4] They attract representatives from all persuasions. It is fitting, therefore, that this book relies on materials and scholarship from all persuasions. And fitting too that its conclusions are supported by some from all persuasions. The book and its thesis are not confessional and not meant to be. They are meant to be persuasive and true. Let readers, whatever their religious convictions, make assessment accordingly.

---

[4] Dennis Barton, *The Clementine Gospel Tradition*, lists the following scholars, with their religious allegiance, who support the traditional dating and authorship of the Gospels: Henry Owen (Anglican), J.J. Griesbach (Lutheran), H.U. Meijboom (Lutheran), J. Chapman (Catholic), B.C. Butler (Catholic), W.R. Farmer (Methodist), J.J. Kiweit (Calvinist), E.R. Richards (Baptist), L. Johnson (Catholic), John Robinson (Anglican), Harold Riley (Anglican), and Bernard Orchard (Catholic). Barton's work was published online in an updated version in 2017 at: http://www.churchinhistory. org/pages/book-clementine-tradition-edited-version/The-Clementine-Gospel-Tradition-by-Dennis-Barton-edited-version.pdf

CHAPTER 1

THE EXISTENTIAL CONTEXT

Section 1: Existential History

The historical critical method as standardly practiced is not so much historical as ideological (the fact will be established in chapter 2). But ideology and dependence on it to resist historical facts in the matter of the Gospels are neither eliminable nor surprising. The Gospels, if historically true, present a challenge to every man about his life, his origin, and his destiny. The challenge is uncomfortable and it provokes to all kinds of excuses to gain escape. Ideology, or systems of ideas that, while powerfully self-reinforcing, rest on flimsy foundations and faulty logic, are the escape favored by the learned (cruder escapes are also available, as alternatives or supplements).

But the Gospel challenge remains. To accept it is indeed to embrace the promise of liberation from sin and death, but it is also to be committed to a way of life and a conviction of judgment that the spirit of the world will always reject. By the spirit of the world is meant the preference for temporal goods, for wealth, fame, power, and the immediate pleasures that bring release from pain. We are material creatures and creature-comforts have an immediate attraction and fascination for us. But they are frequently deceptive, and discipline and self-control are needed to resist the deceit. To accept the truth of the Gospels is to take up the cross daily – the cross not so much of other people as of oneself.

Such inwardly generated hostility to the Gospel and its message is as explicable by human passions as it is predicted by the Gospel itself. In a way, then, we could say that the historical critical method (as far as it purports to be history) was predictable from the beginning. For indeed it happened from the beginning.

When St. Paul preached the resurrection of Christ at Athens he was mocked and few believed him, even though he could and did give eye-witness evidence in its favor (*Acts* 17:30-33). What people objected to was not only the resurrection as a real fact (for daily experience was contrary), but also reformation of life. The moral message of the Gospel was, to be sure, not new. Philosophers and even the higher elements of pagan religion also taught the like, for they taught virtue and self-discipline and restraint of passion. Philosophers and pagans also taught a judgment after death, though admixed with elements of multiple lives and multiple deaths (as in Plato's myths and Hindu and Buddhist beliefs). The historical and therewith theological message of the Gospel, however, was new. It taught the Incarnation along with the Resurrection and a final judgment of all men by the man who had been Resurrected.

Fear of judgment for evil done in life (from which no one is free save by divine grace) makes people deny it, for if judgment does not exist there is no reason to fear it, as the Epicureans taught.[5] To deny judgment is to deny a just God who exacts judgment, or to deny a God who cannot be bought off by gifts and sacrifices but only placated by conversion of life. Old Cephalus in Plato's *Republic* perhaps manifests the phenomenon – a man who had grown rich, perhaps by not altogether worthy means, and, now close to natural death, sought to escape his fears by sacrifice to the gods. His son, Polemarchus, young, not expecting death, and not too particular perhaps about how his father acquired wealth, had no such

---

[5] For example, Lucretius *On the Nature of Things* IV.1090-1104, in *Titi Lucreti Cari, De Rerum Natura Libri Sex*, 2 vols., ed. Cyril Bailey, (Oxford: Oxford University Press, 1947).

qualms. He could listen with more equanimity to the insistent moral probings of Socrates.[6]

The things that thus make men oppose the Gospel message – escape from the fear of death, love of wealth, love of fame, power, and pleasure – are summed by St. John as the desire of the flesh, the desire of the eyes, the pride of life (*1 John* 2:16). The Gospel calls to conversion from all three. The men of Athens who heard St. Paul preach and rejected what he preached are representative of us all. It is in the light of this existential reality, and indeed paradox, of human life that the question of the historicity of the Gospels must be seen if the controversies about them are to be understood. The historical critical method, for all its professed scientific objectivity, is as suffused, if in unacknowledged ways, by the anxious existentialities of human life as the writings of Camus or Sartre.[7]

This point about existentiality can be expanded to cover all history and all concern with history. For by history we mean at least two things. First, we mean all the things that have happened, from the trivial to the important, from the personal to the foreign, from the ordinary to the exotic. What I had for breakfast this morning and whether I brushed my teeth last night are matters of history, as are also who won an election and how damaging a tsunami was and what ancient temple was found beneath the desert sands. But the trivial and ordinary happenings, especially those that happen to most people most of the time, are forgotten or ignored, even by the protagonists, almost as soon as they happen. A Pepys might record them in his diary, and a Proust might make his novel out of them, but these exceptional cases prove the general rule: most of what happens disappears from memory as quickly as it disappears from

---

6   Plato. *Republic*, 328c5-336a10 in *Platonis Opera*, Vol.IV, ed. John Burnet (Oxford: Oxford Classical Texts, 1902).

7   See the quote from Meier at the beginning of the third section of this chapter below, and Bultmann's concern with how to preach an effective summons to the modern mind, in Karl Jaspers and Rudolph Bultmann, *Myth and Christianity. An Inquiry into the Possibility of Religion without Myth* (New York: Noonday Press, Farrar, Strauss and Giroux, 1958), 60-61.

the present moment. The loss of such history causes neither harm nor concern.

The other sense of history, the sense we typically mean by the term, is not all the things that happen but the few things among what happens that dedicated men choose to record and write down. Herodotus, the reputed father of history in this sense, has the original use of the term. His history is expressly a *historie*, by which he means what the Greek word itself first means, namely an investigation.[8] In Herodotus' case it is an investigation into the causes of the wars between the Persians and the Greeks, and it records all the words and deeds it does record in the service of such investigation. These wars were great and stirring events in ancient Greece, and Herodotus chose to investigate them precisely for that reason. Thucydides does the same for the wars between the Athenians and the Spartans in his history, and he chose these wars too because of the great movement in human affairs that they proved to be. Thucydides expressly understood his history as "a possession for ever," because it told through particular happenings universal truths about the human things, the human condition.[9] Livy and Tacitus do something similar for their histories of Rome, and Mercy Otis Warren, to come to more recent times, does the same for the American Revolution.[10]

History in this sense of recording and writing down great events, which is the most common, is a conscious human act undertaken by deliberate choice. It is therefore an act undertaken in view of some good. It is also an act about acts, or about things done by and to men. It is an act, therefore, that is doubly focused on the human good – the good the

---

[8] Herodotus, *Histories* 1.1, in *Herodoti Historiae*, Volume 1, Books I-IV, ed. Charles Hude (Oxford: Oxford Classical Texts, 1908).

[9] Thucydides *Histories* 1.1-2, 22, in *Thucydidis Historiae*, ed. Henry Stuart Jones (Oxford: Oxford Classical Texts, 1942).

[10] Livy, *History of Rome, Preface*, in Titi Livii *Ab Urbe Condita* vol.1, eds. Robert Seymour Conway and Charles Flamstead Walters (Oxford: Oxford Classical Texts, 1914). Tacitus *Historiarum Libri*, ed. C.D. Fisher (Oxford: Oxford Classical Texts, 1911), 1.1. Warren, Mercy Otis, *History of the Rise, Progress and Termination of the American Revolution* (Boston: E. Larkin, 1805), 1.iii-viii.

historian had in view in his writing, and the good the men he writes about had in view in their acting.

Now the men and the acts recorded, and the actual recording itself, are particulars, not universals. They point, or can point, to universals insofar as the particulars are exemplary and display in themselves and their causes universal features of human life. Such at any rate is what Thucydides thought, and Herodotus too. A history, as focused on particulars, is not properly a science, but it can be preparatory to science, for it is preparatory to the science of the human good, or of what is really worth doing, namely the science of ethics and politics and ultimately theology. What men do and what they suffer because of what they do, and what doings and sufferings other men take it upon themselves to record and write down, because they all do it for the sake of some good, tell us about the good they do these things for. History is a chosen human good about other chosen human goods, the goods that men choose to live and die for. It is an existential act about existential acts. Even histories that are mere collections of data, or mere chronicles of things done, are existential, though without the intensity of focus on the human drama that one finds in Thucydides or Herodotus.

Section 2: The Existential Gospels

Some histories focus chiefly on great deeds, as the Persian or Peloponnesian Wars. Others focus chiefly on great men, as Plutarch does in his *Parallel Lives*.[11] But a life is not great without great deeds, and great deeds are not done without great men. And neither men nor deeds are great without great goods being won or lost. Plutarch speaks of great deeds as much as Thucydides and Herodotus speak of great men. The phenomenon is

---

[11] Plutarch *Vitae Parallelae*, eds. Claus Lindskog and Konrat Ziegler (Leipzig: Teubner 1959-1980). An interesting comparison between the Gospels and Plutarch's lives can be found in Michael R. Licona, *Why are there Differences in the Gospels? What we can Learn from Ancient Biography* (Oxford: Oxford University Press, 2017).

universal, and other cultures and peoples have produced their great deeds and men and histories.

It is in the context of what is meant by history in this sense, namely that it is an existential act about existential acts, that any study of the Gospels must be placed. For, without begging questions about their historicity and authenticity, the Gospels come to us as records of a great man and great deeds. Indeed, they come to us as records of a supernaturally great man and supernaturally great deeds. This supernatural dimension is what leads many, of course, to say they are not histories. But that they have this dimension, and what they accordingly say about the great man, make the Gospels more intensely existential, for reader and writer, than Thucydides or Herodotus or Plutarch. They raise, in the most pressing form, the most pressing of existential questions: "where do we come from, what are we, where are we going?"[12]

For this reason, the most pressing question that the Gospels force us to ask about the Gospels is precisely the question of their truth and authenticity. Are the writers reliable eyewitnesses? Is what the great man says, about us and about himself, true? All other questions about the Gospels are secondary and subordinate to this question of their truth. If we are indeed able to decide that the Gospels are not true, or not fully or not literally, because not authentic, we might, for diversion or in an idle hour, investigate their real provenance or their composition. But if we so divert ourselves without deciding the question of truth, or if we decide this question on irrelevant or partisan grounds, as the Athenians did about Paul, we have as much missed or distorted the point as they did.

The present book rests on the truth that the truth of the Gospels as authentic, historical records is the most important fact about them. If they are not such records we may ignore them or put them on a par with poetic imaginings like Ovid's *Metamorphoses* or J. K. Rowling's *Harry Potter*. If they are such records, they command the whole of all our lives, past, present, and future, and transcend in importance everything else

---

[12] The questions, originally written in French, come from the title of a famous painting by Paul Gauguin.

combined. Only from this perspective, the existential perspective, which is the true and human perspective, can the Gospels be properly assessed as the records they claim to be. What value they may otherwise have, as literature, or rhetoric, or religious curiosity, pales by comparison.

Of course, one may, and should, make the same argument about other religious documents, as the Qur'an or the Vedas, namely that what matters in their case too is the truth, the truth about the message they contain, and so about the history they contain that is integral to the message (as it is in the case of the Gospels). Here, though, the focus is the Gospels, and not just because of personal choice or commitment, but because of a certain, but not exclusive, presumptive priority. If the Gospels are historical documents and true, they become the measure for all other religious documents – not for dismissing them (since these other documents may also contain truth), but for qualifying and contextualizing them. Let the same be said of the Qur'an or the Vedas, and let others who, by happenstance of birth or predilection, start there pursue the same search for truth in the same way and with the same motive.

Section 3: Unexistential Gospel Analysis

John P. Meier, who is one of the more prolific and learned of contemporary devotees of the historical critical method as applied to the Gospels, would seem to accept the bearing of the above argument about the existentiality of history. At any rate at the beginning of his multi-volume work, which is as comprehensive in its modern scholarship and its coverage of the Gospel material as one could wish, he speaks in the following way:

> There are certain great questions that each human being has to work out for himself or herself. We learn from past quests, to be sure, but we cannot substitute the lessons of others for our own personal wrestling with the central problems of life...the

unexamined life is not worthy living, and we cannot pay someone else to take it for us.

If this be true of every person's need to search for answers
about the nature of truth, the reality of God, the meaning of
life and death, and what may lie beyond, it is also true of every
Christian's need to search for answers about the reality and meaning of the man named Jesus...[13]

The existential sentiment here is compelling, but Meier seems not
to carry it through. He does say that, in view of Jesus' impact on all of
Western civilization (why only Western, for the impact was worldwide,
even from the beginning?), no person or no religious person can be considered educated who has not investigated to some degree what historical
research can tell us about Jesus.[14] One would therefore expect Meier to
provide the necessary research, and in all its existential urgency too. He
does indeed provide research but in a peculiar way and with no little existential loss. For he proceeds to set out a strange understanding of history
and a strange method of historical research.[15]

The understanding of history is that no history of anyone is possible.
The reason is that there is a difference between the "real" person and the
"historical" person. The total reality of a person, he says, is in principle
unknowable, because all historical knowledge about human persons is
limited by the nature of the case. We can have more or less of such knowledge, and considerable amounts in the case of modern times, where for
instance we may have live recordings of what people say, as with the noto-
rious Watergate tapes, or actual movies of what they said and did. In the
case of some ancient figures, like Cicero, we have their own writings as
well as many letters. But in Jesus' case we have nothing comparable. The

---

[13] John P. Meier *A Marginal Jew. Rethinking the Historical Jesus*, vol.1 (London: Doubleday, 1991), 4.

[14] Meier, *A Marginal Jew*, 1.4

[15] The first point is dealt with here, and the second in the first section of the next chapter.

historical Jesus, the Jesus portrayed in the Gospels, may give us fragments of the "real" person but nothing more. The Gospels, he says, do not portray, and do not claim to portray, the real Jesus with the full range of everything he ever said or did in public or before his disciples in private.[16]

One wonders what the point of the remark is. Would we only know the "real" Jesus if we knew, among other things, how often he washed his hair or cut his finger nails?

The contrast Meier draws is unreal and makes what one may call a category mistake: the mistake of confusing the different ways things exist and are. A real person, like any real thing, is ontologically multiple, being both substance and accidents, as the metaphysicians say. The accidents are indefinitely large in number since they include even the slightest modifications (how often and how quickly a person breathed in any given minute, for instance). The substance is the primary thing that has the accidents, and it is essentially one and stable.

Each of us is the same substance now as when we were born. But by person we typically mean not just the substance but the character. Character refers to a distinct class of accidents in a substance, namely habits, and habits are stable dispositions of voluntary action, action undertaken for the sake of some good. When we say we know a person well, we do not mean that we have seen or met him on several occasions, but that we have seen or met him sufficiently often and sufficiently long to know his character, that is to say, his settled mind and will (together perhaps with something of his development). The real person is the real character.

One can know the real character, as close friends know each other, without knowing all the details of everything said and done. One can know these details, or many of them, as fans know stars of film or sports, and not know the real character. It is a mistake to think the fan knows the star better than the star's friend just because the fan knows details the friend ignores. The friend knows the character; the fan does not. Meier in

---

[16]   Meier, *A Marginal Jew*, 1.24-25

effect concedes as much when he says that a good deal of the total reality of a person would be irrelevant and positively boring to historians even if it could be known.[17] For the irrelevant and boring can only be judged by reference to some standard of the relevant and interesting, and this standard would ultimately be the existentiality of human life, or its abiding focus on character and action and the good of both.

The mistake in question here is that of putting "real person" into the category of all the accidents instead of into the category of character and the works of character. For it is in fact very easy to know the real person, the real character and deeds, without knowing all or most of the details Meier wants. It is also very easy to depict a real person in words if one knows the character and has the necessary writing skill. Good biographers do it all the time for actual people, and good novelists do the same for imagined ones. The Gospels, the supposed biographies or memoirs of Jesus, do indeed give us the real Jesus, for they give us the character of Jesus and the deeds and words that most display that character. Moreover, if the Gospels are historically accurate, they also give us the historical Jesus, the real Jesus who lived in First Century Palestine. For Meier's differentiation of the "real" from the "historical" is as false a dichotomy as his "real person" is a false category. If a real person can be known, a historical person can be known, and for this purpose all one needs is personal acquaintance, either directly oneself or indirectly through others who had direct personal acquaintance and handed on accurate reports.

The conclusion to draw would thus seem to be that the problem of the historicity of the Gospels cannot even be posed, let alone solved, in the way people like Meier set it up. Those who distinguish the real Jesus from the historical Jesus, or even the Jesus of faith from the Jesus of history, have failed to take seriously the existentiality of history and indeed of human life as such. The concern with the good, our own and that of others, which motivates both history and the writing of it, cannot, if taken seriously, lead to any notion of "real" or "historical" divorced from

---

[17] Meier, *A Marginal Jew*, 1.24.

character and from the goodness and badness of character. The person is the character, and the character is the real person, and the real person is the person of history, and, if the person of history deserves to be believed in or trusted in some way, the person of history is the person of faith. There is no rupture here; there is seamless continuity.

Indeed, without such seamless continuity, the problem posed by the distinction between "real" and "historical" and "faith" would seem to be intractable. For if Jesus is really the Messiah and Son of God, how else would he manifest the fact to his contemporaries except by speaking and acting as the Gospels show him speaking and acting? And how else would his contemporaries report this fact except by writing what and how they did? To suppose, on the grounds that the Gospels show a Jesus who manifests himself as God, that the Gospels are not historical eyewitness reports is to assume a priori that Jesus did not manifest himself as God. Indeed, it is to impose an impossible condition: either Jesus manifested himself as God or he did not; if he did not, he did not; if he did, he was not a historical figure (such manifestation is historically impossible); so in either event he did not manifest himself as God.

This way of arguing is parallel to saying that the Gospel writers cannot be trusted when they portray Jesus as God because they were Christians and so biased, and that someone who was not a Christian and portrayed Jesus as God (Josephus perhaps?[18]) cannot be trusted because he did not believe what he said. In either event, whether he is a Christian or not, or whether he believes what he said or not, no one who says Jesus was God can be believed. These ways of arguing are perverse. They render it logically impossible *ab initio* for God incarnate ever to be known as God incarnate. One wonders why God would bother – or why or how anyone could believe.

---

[18]   See the discussion of Josephus in section 2 of chapter 4 below.

CHAPTER 2

THE METHOD OF HISTORY

Section 1: An Instructive Example

If Meier and others have misunderstood history, one would expect them also to misunderstand the method of history. The method they adopt goes by the name, as already remarked, of the historical critical method, which is sometimes also glossed as the method of scientific history, or the method of history in the modern sense.[19] What is actually meant by this method is not easy to pin down. In what follows, therefore, the method adopted by Meier will first be discussed. The reason for beginning with Meier is that his book is clear, recent, up to date in its scholarship, and nicely representative of the whole historical critical school. However other accounts of the method and other examples will follow later to give a fair overview of the general thing.

To begin with, note that Meier does not think the Gospels count as history in the modern sense of the word, because they aim to proclaim and strengthen faith in Jesus as Son of God, Lord, and Messiah.[20] This judgment reflects Meier's false distinction between the real Jesus,

---

[19] History in this sense is apparently not earlier than the Enlightenment: Meier, *A Marginal Jew*, 1.25.

[20] Meier, *A Marginal Jew*, 1.40.

the historical Jesus, and the Jesus of faith. It also reflects his failure to follow through on the existentiality of history. Meier holds also the standard view in New Testament research today[21] that Mark, using oral and perhaps written traditions, comes first and was written about 70AD; that Matthew and Luke, working independently of each other, wrote longer Gospels between 70 and 100AD based partly on Mark, partly on a collection of sayings called Q, and partly on special traditions peculiar to each; while John follows an independent tradition.

This view of the Gospels, widely accepted though it be, ignores and is in conflict with the extrinsic historical evidence about the Gospels. It is based solely on internal literary-critical analysis of the Gospels themselves. That it is thus not a historical view is evident on its face. That it is in addition an arbitrary and logically incoherent view will be argued later when the extrinsic historical evidence is itself discussed. What is of concern now is the way Meier seeks to extract a history of Jesus from literary-critical analysis, for his way has special peculiarities of its own.[22] Since Meier distinguishes the Jesus of faith from the Jesus of history (and also from the real Jesus), and since the Gospels are shot through with proclamation of the Jesus of faith and are, according to Meier, products of Christian churches in the latter half of the first century AD, he contends that only a careful examination of the Gospel material in the light of the criteria of historicity can give us reliable results as to the Jesus of history.

For this purpose Meier imagines an "unpapal" conclave of a Catholic, a Protestant, a Jew, and an agnostic (but not, it seems, a Muslim or a Buddhist) being forced to hammer out, on the basis of the relevant criteria, a consensus document about Jesus. This image of an unpapal conclave, while colorful enough, is essentially tangential to what Meier does. What matters are the relevant criteria, the "criteria of historicity,"

---

[21] Meier, *A Marginal Jew*, 1.43-44.

[22] Meier, *A Marginal Jew*, 2.4-6.

through which what most likely belongs to the Jesus of history is to be determined by the conclave, or indeed by anyone. The criteria are five.[23]

First is the criterion of embarrassment, which pinpoints material the early Church would not have invented because it caused embarrassment or theological difficulty. Second is the criterion of discontinuity, which focuses on words and deeds of Jesus that cannot be derived from contemporary Judaism or the early Church. Third is the criterion of multiple attestation, which focuses on words and deeds of Jesus found in more than one independent source (to wit, Mark, Q, Paul, John) or in more than one form (parable, miracle story, etc.). Fourth is the criterion of coherence, which accepts as historical other words and deeds of Jesus that cohere with those that meet the preceding criteria. Fifth is the criterion of Jesus' rejection, trial, and execution, which looks for words and deeds of Jesus that, because of how they threatened or alienated people, could serve to explain those events.

As an example of something that meets the first criterion Meier gives the baptism of Jesus by John. As an example of something that meets the second he gives Jesus' rejection of voluntary fasting. As an example of something that meets the third Meier gives Jesus' prohibition of divorce, and the repute Jesus had in his own lifetime of, for example, giving sight to the blind.

What is remarkable about these criteria is not so much how few they are (though their fewness is odd) but how unhistorical they are (with the exception of the fifth, to be dealt with shortly). Indeed, these limited criteria are only justifiable, if they are justifiable, because of the distinction between the real Jesus, the historical Jesus, and the Jesus of faith. The Jesus of faith is the Jesus worshipped in the early Church, and the Gospels, which were produced by the early Church, are judged to be altogether reflective of that worship (instead of that worship to be altogether reflective of the Gospels). The Jesus of history, therefore, can only be

---

[23] Meier, *A Marginal Jew, ibid.*; more fully at 1.1-2, 168-177.

determined reliably by those elements of the Gospels that are somehow separable from the Jesus of faith.

Of such sort are elements that are in tension with or at a tangent to the Jesus of faith so that faith could not explain them, or that are so deeply embedded in the Gospel tradition that only something real could explain them. But not only does this view depend on a rejection of the historical evidence about the origin of the Gospels (a point to be returned to), it also limits the science of history to an unjustifiably thin and arbitrary basis. Historical documents are not to be judged reliable because they fit these sort of criteria but because they fit other criteria, as that they come from people who were in a position to know the facts recorded (as eyewitnesses or as relying on eyewitnesses), who are known not to be willful liars or deliberate distorters of such facts (and Meier's and other scholars' early Church, which produced the Gospels, is presumed, if only methodologically, to have been such a distorter), who accurately report things known to be true from other and independent sources (other historians, contemporary documents, archaeological discoveries), who know things, especially incidental things, that only an eyewitness could have known, and the like.

This point can be given some confirmation from Meier's fifth criterion, which, while historical as far as it goes, assumes independently the historicity of Jesus' trial and execution. But why assume that Jesus was tried and crucified?[24] The only answer can be that the evidence from the relevant historical documents is reliable. The relevant historical documents are the Gospels themselves and the New Testament letters. Mentions in other documents (Tacitus, for instance, or Josephus[25]) are derivative and later than the late date scholars give to the Gospels, or at least later than Mark. But if we can trust the Gospels about the trial and crucifixion, why not also about the resurrection, or indeed about other things the Gospels

---

[24] Some early heretics denied the crucifixion of Jesus, and Islam still does.

[25] Tacitus, *Annals*, ed. C.D. Fisher (Oxford: Oxford Classical Texts, 1906), 15.44; Josephus, *Antiquities of the Jews* ed. B. Niese (Berlin: Weidmann, 1892), 18.3.3.

say? Should the answer be that the trial and crucifixion fit the other criteria, the claim is false. The trial and crucifixion do not embarrass the early Church because they are required for the resurrection, and the resurrection, already in the letters of St. Paul (not to mention his speech at Athens), is the glory of the Church. Neither are they discontinuous with contemporary Judaism, since the slaying of blasphemers (which Jesus was accused of being) is in continuity with Judaic law. Nor finally can it matter that they are found in more than one independent source, for so is the resurrection which, however, is not supposed to be historical.

Meier and other scholars are forced into their peculiar criteria and away from really historical criteria because of their view about the authorship and dating of the Gospels. Were they to give up that view and follow the external evidence about authorship and dating their problem would dissolve. But they will not give up the view because they accept the historical critical method, which will not give it up. What, then, is that method, and why will it not give up the view in question, for we cannot glean satisfactory answers from the above sort of criteria?

Section 2: The Historical Critical Method

The modern historical critical method has its beginnings in the Enlightenment, according to Meier. He does not, however, give any overview of its origin and development.[26] Other scholars do and have. One of the fullest accounts is given by Law,[27] who even discerns anticipatory elements of the method in Luther and also in some early Christian writers.

---

[26] Meier, A Marginal Jew, 1.25.

[27] David Law, The Historical Critical Method. A Guide for the Perplexed. (New York: Continuum, 2012), 25-80. Also William R. Farmer, The Synoptic Problem. A Critical Analysis. (New York: Macmillan, 1964), 1-198; Orchard, Bernard, Edmund Sutcliffe, et al. A Catholic Commentary on Holy Scripture (London: Thomas Nelson & Sons, 1953) §§604a-609e, pp.752-759; Pontifical Biblical Commission, The Interpretation of the Bible in the Church (1994), I.A.1. At the Holy See, www.vatican.va; Werner G. Kümmel, Introduction to the New Testament. Trans. A.J. Mattill (London: SCM Press, 1966), 37-42.

But these anticipations admittedly concern matters of literary criticism alone, while the method in its developed form rests not only on literary criticism but also and more crucially on a certain scientific rationalism and a certain historical presupposition.

The historical presupposition is that the ancient external evidence about the date and authorship of the Gospels can and should be rejected. The scientific rationalism is that supernatural happenings (miracles, prophecies, exorcisms) are impossible as historical fact and that where they are talked of they are to be regarded as having a mythical or allegorical or theological and not literal meaning. The literary criticism focuses on disparities between or within the Gospels in order to trace out layers of composition and origin.[28] The decisive member among these three is the scientific rationalism, for without it there would be no reason to dismiss the ancient external evidence and little reason to use literary criticism for purposes of literary dismantling. Treatment of it will, in addition, enable one better to see what the proper study of history requires and what it does not require.

Section 3: Rejection of the Supernatural

Some brief mention of the use of literary criticism has been given already with reference to Meier's un-existential method, and more will be given in the next chapter. The ancient external evidence will also be dealt with later, in chapter 4, because of certain particular questions that it raises. Here the scientific rationalism will be reviewed and examined, and it is best to begin with a few apposite quotes. Law, for instance, notes the following about some of the early proponents of the historical critical method:

> The problem of historical improbability becomes even more acute with those biblical accounts that describe supernatural occurrences. To the modern reader whose understanding of the

---

[28] Orchard and Sutcliffe, *Catholic Commentary on Holy Scripture* §§609d-e, p.759.

world has been molded by the natural sciences, biblical accounts of prophetic visions, miracles, visitations by angels and demonic possession seem inherently implausible.[29]

He also quotes de Wette, for whom the credibility of the report and the historicity of the events it relates must be placed in doubt if the report contains miraculous elements such as God or angels speaking directly to human beings, or when it describes events which violate general human experience or the laws of nature.[30] According to David Strauss, whom Law also cites, taking supernatural events to be historical demands belief in the incredible. In view of our knowledge of how the world works we cannot take, for example, Jesus' walking on the water as literally true.[31] Again, according to a citation from Pfleiderer:

> If Christianity relies on the Incarnation and miracles, then the origin of Christianity is a complete miracle that escapes all historical explanation. For understanding a phenomenon historically means understanding its causal connection with the circumstances obtaining at a particular time and place in human life.[32]

Pfleiderer's aim was to interpret the history of Christianity according to the same principles and methods as any other history. The only presuppositions he accepted were the analogy of human experience or the likeness of human nature in past and present, and the causal connection of all external events and all internal spiritual experience, or in brief the regular order of the world, which has determined all human experience for all time.[33]

---

[29] Law, *Historical Critical Method*, 2.

[30] Law, *Historical Critical Method*, 53-54.

[31] Law, *Historical Critical Method*, 59.

[32] Law, *Historical Critical Method*, 68.

[33] Law, *Historical Critical Method*, 68.

A quotation from Rudolph Bultmann proves the same:

Both the legend of the empty tomb and the appearances insist on the physical reality of the risen body of the Lord .... But these are almost certainly later embellishments of the primitive tradition. St. Paul knows nothing about them. There is however one passage where Paul tries to prove the miracle of the resurrection by adducing a list of eye-witnesses (*1 Corinthians* 15:3-8). But this is a dangerous procedure... An historical fact which involves a resurrection from the dead is utterly inconceivable.[34]

Or again:

He [Karl Jaspers] is as convinced as I am that a corpse cannot come back to life or rise from the grave, that there are no demons and no magic causality.[35]

A further and more extended quotation from Christian Hartlich on the historical critical method is even more enlightening. He gives as one of his theses for the method the following:

Sacred history is characterized by the fact that beings which are not ascertainable in the context of ordinary experience, beings of divine, demonic, and supernatural origin, are active in an otherwise empirical and natural sequence of events. Statements concerning such sacred history are fundamentally unverifiable, and in this sense, from the perspective of that which has in fact taken place, without value for the historian.[36]

---

[34] Rudolph Bultmann (and five critics) *Kerygma and Myth*, ed. Hans Werner Bartsch, trans. Reginald H. Fuller (New York: Harper and Row, 1961), 39.

[35] Jaspers and Bultmann, *Myth and Christianity*, 60-61.

[36] Christian Hartlich, 'Historisch-kritische Methode in ihrer Anwendung auf Geschehnisaussagen der Hl. Schrift,' *Zeitschrift für Theologie und Kirche* 75, (1978),

In illustration he takes a verse from Matthew about the great earthquake that happened when the women came to Jesus' tomb, for an angel of the Lord descended from heaven and came and rolled back the stone, and sat upon it (*Matthew* 28:2). Hartlich comments:

> The earthquake referred to here is an event whose factuality we are fundamentally able to verify, perhaps by means of some ascertainable effect. In principle, we therefore have at our disposal the stipulations by means of which the statement that there and then an earthquake took place can be tested with regard to its truth. When in the same narrative, however, the descent of an angel from heaven is given as the cause of the earthquake, this is a statement regarding an event for which every determination of truth or falsehood is fundamentally withdrawn. For the assertion that an angel descended from heaven refers not merely to the descent of a being of a certain appearance, ascertainable by our senses (his appearance was like lightning, and his raiment white as snow); this assertion refers also to the descent of a being of supernatural origin and supernatural character, a heavenly being, in the sense of a being having been sent from God and acting in his service and with his authority. In all these respects, however, an angel as such is fundamentally removed from every verification.[37]

This comment by Hartlich is thoroughly unhistorical and against the rules of empirical knowledge. Nothing prevents a supernatural event from happening or from being made empirically manifest, and so from being empirically known and empirically verified.[38] To say otherwise is a mere

---

467-484, monograph 2. Translated by Darrell J. Doughty, https://depts.drew.edu/jhc/hartlich.html

[37] *Ibid.*, monograph 2.

[38] For more direct discussion of the historicity in principle of miracles see the section on Hume below.

posit which cannot be defended on empirical grounds. Supernatural happenings are not impossible (there is nothing contradictory about them), and so they cannot be ruled out in principle or a priori. Or they could only be ruled out in principle and a priori if the existence of a supernatural power capable of causing a supernatural event could be ruled out in principle and a priori.

There are philosophies that deny the existence of the supernatural, but then the ruling out of supernatural events is made on philosophical and not on empirical or historical grounds. Further, these philosophical grounds are false. Nothing in logic proves the impossibility of the supernatural, for the supernatural is not self-contradictory. Nothing in physical science proves it, for physical science expressly limits itself as a matter of method to natural things that are naturally explicable, and does not say, nor can it say, that there are no supernatural things. All it can say in face of a supernatural event is that there is no natural explanation. Jesus' walking on the water, for example (*Matthew* 14:22-33), has no natural explanation. Heavy bodies sink in water; they are not held up by it on the surface. The disciples were good natural scientists here, because their immediate reaction was that they were seeing a ghost or spirit, for spirits have no weight. They were only convinced it was not a spirit but the bodily Jesus himself when Jesus made it clear to them who he was and when indeed Peter too, at Jesus' command, started walking on the water. Nothing, finally, in history proves the impossibility of the supernatural, for history is empirically open and if a supernatural event is empirically manifest, as Jesus' walking on the water was made manifest to the disciples, it is thereby also a fact of history.

Philosophy can only rule out the supernatural by laying down as one of its suppositions, or as an implication of one of its suppositions, that the supernatural does not exist. But such laying down will be a mere posit or methodological assumption. It will not be proof. Bultmann illustrates the assumption when he says that, while scholars should not presuppose their results, there is nevertheless one presupposition that cannot be dismissed, namely that:

[H]istory is a unity in the sense of a closed continuum of effects… This closedness means that the continuum of historical happenings cannot be rent by the interference of supernatural, transcendent powers, and that therefore there is no "miracle" in this sense of the word.[39]

Rejecting the supernatural in this way is arbitrary prejudice, and without warrant. Bultmann himself proves as much when he writes, "We cannot use electric lights and radios and…avail ourselves of modern medical and clinical means and at the same time believe in the spirit and wonder world of the New Testament."[40] For, as Meier rightly points out,[41] opinion surveys show that very many people today use modern technology and believe in miracles. Perhaps such persons are being inconsistent (which may be Bultmann's point), but as a matter of empirical fact belief in miracles is no less possible now than it was in the times of the New Testament.

More relevant, however, is that rejecting the supernatural even goes against the physical science on which Bultmann in particular relies for support of his view that supernatural happenings must be excluded from any account of historical fact. For, first, science is an investigation of natural things through their natural causes, and since supernatural things by definition lack a natural cause, they escape the limits and the competence of the scientific method.

To retort, second, that nothing happens that can in principle escape the limits and competence of the scientific method is not to make a statement within science but a statement about science. So it is not to make a statement whose truth can be determined by science. Science and its method are not something that scientific investigation investigates (by

---

[39] Rudolph Bultmann, *Existence and Faith: Short Writings of Rudolph Bultmann*, ed. and trans. Schubert M. Ogden (New York: World, 1966), 289-291.

[40] Rudolph Bultmann, *New Testament and Mythology and other Basic Writings*, ed. and trans. Schubert M. Ogden (Fortress Press, 1989), 4.

[41] Meier, *A Marginal Jew*, 2.520-521

putting it in a test tube, say, or under a microscope), but something that scientific investigation uses. Statements about the method of science belong to the philosophy of science, and it is evident from the philosophy of science that neither science nor its method says that science deals with everything that happens or can happen, but only that it deals with everything that happens through natural causes. If something happens through supernatural causes, science simply says nothing (other than recording the fact), for it is not equipped to say anything. A scientific and empirical investigation of an alleged miraculous happening may indeed conclude that the happening in fact has a natural cause (and so is not miraculous). But it may equally well conclude that it does not have a natural cause, in which case it says nothing further about the cause (though it does not deny that there must be one).[42]

Third, science is empirical and follows the facts whatever they are found to be. So, if some facts are found to be miraculous or to lack a natural cause, then science must allow that some things lack natural causes, or in other words that not everything can be explained by the natural causes that alone fall within its competence.

For note, fourth, that the science of physics in particular considers only what can be measured by experiments under controlled conditions, and so too only what can be repeatedly measured by others who conduct the same experiments; and this method manifestly does not apply to historical events like miracles, which are singular facts and not repeatedly measurable in controlled experiments.

Fifth, even what is measured in controlled experiments does not establish that only what can thus be measured is possible or real, but only that what can be measured in controlled experiments can be measured in controlled experiments and can be used for purposes of scientific explanation.

---

[42] While natural science is thus incompetent to investigate supernatural causes, neither it nor scientists deny the need for causes. The search for causes is of the essence of natural science as it is of any science, and if natural science determines that some event has no natural cause, it has thereby determined that it has a supernatural cause. What it does not determine is the who or what or why of this supernatural cause.

A miracle, of course, is not a controlled experiment but a supernatural event, so that the method of physics is of necessity not applicable to it.

Sixth, to demand that miracles, in order to count as real, must be subject to measurement in controlled experiments commits the fallacy of *petitio principii*. It assumes the impossibility of miracles to prove the impossibility of miracles. A miracle is a particular supernatural or divine act, dependent on the voluntary determination of a supernatural or divine power, and such voluntary determinations are not things subject to measurable repetition in controlled experiments. The point is not that miracles are inexplicable or that they follow no rules, but that the explanation and the rules are beyond the reach of natural science. They are doubtless not beyond supernatural science, but supernatural science is certainly beyond natural science.

Seventh, if some other science is appealed to, as the science of logic, then this science does not exclude miracles. It only excludes logical impossibilities or things happening with no sufficient reason, and miracles are not logical impossibilities but natural impossibilities, or impossibilities that, while impossible for natural power, are not impossible for the supernatural power that does sufficiently explain them. Further, logic says nothing about whether there is or is not a supernatural power, nor does physics. The former confines itself to principles of thought and the latter to measurable quantities, so that, of set profession, neither is competent to determine the existence or non-existence of supernatural powers.

Eighth, if the science appealed to is the science of history, there is nothing in this kind of science that rules out miracles, since there is nothing in it that determines in advance what can or cannot happen. History bases itself on what did happen, and since from what did happen the inference to what can happen is valid, if a miracle happened then miracles can happen, and there is nothing in history or the science of history to oppose this conclusion.

Ninth if the science appealed to is the philosophy of religion, there is nothing here either that rules out miracles because there is nothing here that rules out the existence of a god or supernatural power that could or would intervene in the world to perform them. Despite the number of contemporary philosophers who deny the existence of a personal and providential God, none would assert that they have irrefutable proof for their denial. They assert rather that their denial is more plausible or better founded, or the like, than the contrary assertion. But only if an irrefutable proof were forthcoming could one be certain, in advance of examining the empirical facts, that miracles and the like supernatural events do not happen or have never happened. Accordingly, one cannot, on this basis, rule out a priori the truth of empirical reports about the real happening of such things. One must instead examine the reports directly and according to the criteria proper for deciding any empirical question. And if any such reports turn out to be true, they will constitute evidence for the existence of a miracle-causing God.

Section 4: Empirical Fact and the Supernatural

One cannot, to escape this consequence, appeal to the celebrated philosophical argument of Hume against miracles,[43] for this argument is multiply defective.

First Hume defines a miracle as a transgression of a natural law. This definition is wrong because no natural law states as part of itself that it operates in the presence of a supernatural power. It states only that in operates in the presence of natural powers. But a miracle is by supposition the work of supernatural power. A miracle does not transgress natural law, therefore, but is rather the exercise of a higher power. It is not unlike the way we "transgress" the law of gravity when we pick a stone off the

---

[43] David Hume, *An Enquiry Concerning Human Understanding* (Indianapolis: Hackett, 1993), section 10. The criticisms of Hume's argument given here are only a few of the more telling that can be leveled against it. For a very extensive discussion of the question of miracles and their evidence and credibility see Horne *A Summary of the Evidence for the Genuineness, Authenticity, etc. of the Holy Scriptures* (London: Longman, 1861), 203-270, and on Hume in particular, 211-214, 265-270. It is available online through Google books. Meier has a brief discussion of problems with the argument, *A Marginal Jew* 1.530-531 n.31.

ground. By itself a stone will not rise. In the presence of a human being, who has power over a stone greater than gravity has, it can rise because it rises with the man's hand.

Consequently, and second, because miracles do not transgress natural law, Hume's claim that a witness to a miracle is more likely to be lying than that a natural law has been transgressed, so that the evidence against a miracle is always stronger than the evidence for it, at once falls away. If there is a supernatural power, the evidence of a witness to a miracle performed by such higher power is no less reliable than the evidence of a witness to a purely natural event. All depends on the standard conditions required for determining if a witness is to be judged reliable, namely whether he was really present at the event, whether he was in a good position to witness it, whether or not he has any strong motive to lie, whether he has proved himself a reliable witness on other occasions, whether his testimony stands up to cross examination and the like. Since the witnesses for at least some miracles seem to meet these conditions (as even Hume allows in the passage referred to), their existence can hardly with reason be denied.[44]

Finally, Hume's argument is only an epistemological and not also an ontological one. It does not tell us about what can happen but only about what we could be in a position to know happened. So, if it works at all, it leaves open the possibility of miracles and rules out only our knowing the reality of them. But in fact it does not rule out our knowing the reality either, for Hume's empiricism requires us to follow the empirical data for our knowledge of what happens, and the empirical data are for too numerous to be fully known by anyone. They are too numerous ever to found necessary laws as opposed to presumptive ones, and presumptive laws by definition allow for exceptions. Add also that reports of supernatural happenings exist in such numbers and come from so many places and times, including present ones, that to suppose they are all lies or false imaginings is more incredible than to suppose some are true.

---

[44] The material in this paragraph is adapted from my *Political Illiberalism. A defense of Freedom* (Routledge, 2017), 75-76. Used with permission.

Empirical experience of human reports, on which we anyway have to rely for knowledge of anything beyond our own very narrow compass, argues that men, even known liars, more often tell the truth than not (after all liars will not, as they wish, get away with their lies if nothing they ever say is true, or if they do not tell the truth most of the time, or if the falsehood of what they say has not even the color of truth). Empirical experience conflicts with, and renders unempirical, any view that would reject all supernatural events always and everywhere. A true empiricism, just as it cannot ontologically rule out the real possibility of miracles, so it cannot epistemologically rule out the real knowledge of them.

Meier's discussion of the historicity of miracles, by contrast, is saner and more measured, but he has a fastidious understanding of what in a supposed miracle can count as history and what cannot. He writes, for instance, the following:

> The historian can ascertain whether an extraordinary event has taken place in a religious setting, whether someone has claimed it to be a miracle, and – if there is enough evidence – whether a human action, physical forces in the universe, misperception, illusion, or fraud can explain the event. If all these explanations are excluded, the historian may conclude that an event claimed by some people to be miraculous has no reasonable explanation or adequate cause in any human activity or physical force. To go beyond that judgment and to affirm either that God has directly acted…or that God has not done so is to go beyond what any historian can affirm in his or her capacity as a historian and to enter the domain of philosophy or theology.[45]

The distinction is overdrawn. The extraordinary event is allowed by Meier to be a historical fact both as to its happening and as to its being beyond natural power, but the identification of its cause as supernatural or divine is not allowed to be historical. However, historians do not

---

[45]   Meier, *A Marginal Jew*, 2.514-515.

give up allegiance to common sense and logic when they do history. In particular they do not give up the principle that events have adequate causes. On the contrary, it is their reliance on this principle that allows them to explain historical events, such as why Napoleon lost the battle of Waterloo. For there is some reason that Napoleon lost and a historian's job is to distinguish causes that could not explain the loss from those that could, and to adjudicate as best he can between them. Mercy Otis Warren, indeed, that remarkable historian of the American Revolution, makes exactly this point:

> History,…requires a just knowledge of character to investigate the causes of action; a clear comprehension to review the combination of causes; and precision of language to detail the events…[46]

So, likewise, in the case of events that are extraordinary. If some such events are beyond natural causes, they must have supernatural ones. Meier's words seem to allow an historian to assert the antecedent of this conditional but not to assert the consequent – for even if an historian cannot affirm that God is the supernatural cause, he must assert that something with the power attributed to God is the cause. But Meier allows an historian to know, as a historian, that some event has no natural cause, so he must allow an historian to know that some event has a supernatural cause. The supernatural cannot therefore be excluded from history and the science of history. To allow that it can be is to allow that things can happen for no reason, which, by removing reason from what happens, removes all human science simply, including the science of history. For science is essentially the search for causes and if causes are not needed or do not exist science is vain.

One cannot avoid this result by saying, as Meier allows an atheist might say,[47] that an alleged miracle must have a natural cause though a

---

[46] Warren, *History*, 1.1

[47] Meier, *A Marginal Jew*, 2.515.

cause we do not yet know. Such a position threatens rapidly to become unempirical, and so unhistorical, because it threatens rapidly to become belief in something not only without evidence but even against evidence (the evidence that in this case there is no natural cause). Such a belief is more a matter of blind faith than a belief in miracles could ever be.[48]

Meier is nevertheless right up to a point. There is a distinction between admitting that some supernatural power is at work and identifying that supernatural power with God, or with the God of the Old and New Testaments. Perhaps there are other supernatural powers, as indeed the pagans believed, who posited many gods. Which supernatural power is at work need not then be deducible from the extraordinary event itself but from the larger context and from what the miracle worker says. The context in Jesus' case is that of the Judeo-Christian God, and what he says shows that the miracles are done by the power of his own name (as the Apostles after him did miracles by the power of his name, *Acts* 3:1-10), all which give sufficient evidence of his divinity. Such facts are as accessible to the historian as any other and ordinary facts. So, if the historian is competent to speak and reason about these ordinary facts, he is competent to speak and reason about the other facts too.

We may confirm this point from what Jesus said to the Pharisees, who did not deny that Jesus had supernatural power to cast out demons (the empirical facts were too evident), but did deny that the supernatural power was God's (*Matthew* 12:22-32, *Mark* 3:20-30). They said instead that it was Satan's. Jesus' response was not to perform another exorcism but to expose the fallacy in the Pharisees' reasoning. Their belief that Satan was using his demonic power to expel demons was incoherent, first because a kingdom divided against itself cannot stand (and Satan's kingdom did stand, for demon possession stood), and second because if Satan

---

[48] The famous empiricist argument against belief in the existence of God, that such belief means maintaining something in such a way that empirical evidence ceases to have any relevance to it (for the belief is compatible with any state of affairs whatever), works just as well against belief in the non-existence of miracles. Antony Flew, Richard. M. Hare, & Basil Mitchell, 'Theology and falsification: the University discussion' in *New Essays in Philosophical Theology* (New York: Macmillan, 1964).

was being deprived of his goods (the people possessed by his demons), a stronger than Satan, namely God, must be there to do the depriving.

The logic of this refutation needs to be taken seriously. For the refutation only works on the supposition that the exercise of supernatural power was a matter of discernible fact. Deny that supposition and the refutation fails. But the Pharisees did not deny it (the empirical reality of what Jesus did was undeniable, as the evidence recorded in the Gospels makes clear). They alleged a different supernatural power. Miracles as manifestations of supernatural power can be as historical as anything else. Identifying the supernatural power in question is also historical, for it is a matter of what the miracle worker does and says, which is historical (as the Pharisees were unable to deny). The rest follows by logical necessity: some supernatural power is at work here (the supernatural character of the effect is plainly observable); the worker of the effect shows the power to be divine (it is greater than Satan's); no other power could do the job; therefore, the effect is a work of divine power. The premises and the inference here are historical or historically based. Nothing more is needed for a miracle to be a historical fact. Meier, for instance, allows historicity to the extraordinary event, but not to the fact it is a miracle, or a work of divine power. He confuses a distinction between premises and conclusion with a distinction between the historical and the non-historical. But the science of history is impossible without the drawing of conclusions from premises.

In short then, and to conclude this stage of the argument, there is nothing in reason or science or fact to establish the rationalist premise of the historical critical method that supernatural events or miracles cannot be historical or part of genuine history.

CHAPTER 3

LITERARY CRITICISM

Section 1: Existential Abstraction

What then of the historical critical method's approach to and use of literary criticism? The first thing to note here is something that was already observed about the rejection of the supernatural, namely a certain abstraction from the existentiality of history. For the rejection of this existentiality was tied to the desire to understand the past as it was, and so as it does not relate, or need not relate, to the existentiality of the researcher and the reader. It was tied to a desire to understand the past simply as past without any necessarily further interest. As Law notes,[49] it was work on the history of Rome that influenced the application of the historical critical method to Biblical interpretation. He mentions Barthold Niebuhr and Leopold von Ranke in particular, and of the latter he writes:

> The work of the historian Leopold von Ranke (1795-1866) was important for laying the foundations of what has come to be known as "historicism." In his *History of the Roman and German Peoples* and subsequent works von Ranke strove to achieve as

---

[49] Law, *Historical Critical Method*, 53

objective a representation of history as possible. In the preface of his book he states as his aim that "he merely wishes to show how it really was." He is not concerned to consider the relevance of historical events for the present, but is concerned solely with a supposedly objective portrayal of the past.

The historical critical method shares this desire to understand "how it really was," and it approaches the literary phenomena of the Gospels with this desire. But such desire, as actually carried through, is defective. Most of all, it can lead to a lack of concern with the existentiality of "how it really was" for the actual participants, even though such existentiality was necessarily an integral part of "how it really was." This lack of concern can, perhaps, be overcome through attention to the *Sitz im Leben* (the "setting in life") of the participants, or of the sources that tell us about them, for the *Sitz im Leben* is the existentiality of the participants. But the lack of concern remains in that their existentiality, while it must be noted, is not something for us ourselves as historians to enter into. We are supposed to view things objectively, which we could not do if we were personally engaged and let their existentiality become in some way our own. But such viewing of things objectively is itself an existential stance, and an existential stance that hides its existentiality behind the objectivity of its object. Our own existentiality is supposed to have no place in the science of history but only, if at all, in something else,[50] and this something else may follow, but need not, the existentially abstracted search.

Not that such abstraction is impossible or entirely lacking in value and utility, but it is an abstraction nevertheless. We all live, however unthinkingly, in and with the question of the meaning of life and all our choices are inevitably engagements with that question. But if one's choice is to abstract from existentiality, one can come to believe that one's choice is as abstract as one has made the object of it to be, and that one's choice thus enjoys the same objectivity as the object. The belief is false

---

[50] For an instance, see Bultmann's summons to modern man, in Jaspers and Bultmann, *Myth and Christianity*, 60-61; also Meier, *A Marginal Jew*, 1.24.

(the choice is not abstract; it is a thoroughly existential engagement), but it can appear true. One can thus be led to embrace an existentiality where the rationality and coherence or otherwise of the presuppositions behind it, because they are not viewed existentially, are unexamined or too little examined. The rejection of the historicity of miracles is the prime case in point. It manifests a "rationalism" that, for all its claim to objectivity, is as existential, as much an engagement with the human condition and its meaning, and as much a commitment to some vision of the good, as a religious commitment or even an anti-religious commitment.

Section 2: Literary Criticism and the Gospels

Turning, however, from this warning back to the historical critical method itself, one may briefly describe the method as one of using literary elements of the text (form and genre in particular) to isolate the sources (written or oral) that were then variously redacted (by some editor) to form the text as we now have it. The material is as such "synchronic," that is, gleaned from the text as it now exists in completed state. The use, however, is "diachronic," that is, directed at uncovering how the material, thus gleaned, came to have through time the synchronic form it now does have.

As to the diachronic part, Law's account is worth summarizing. First, he helpfully notes the prior necessity of textual criticism, which is concerned with establishing as accurate a text as the surviving manuscripts allows us to reach.[51] The point is that the original texts, or autographs as they are called, no longer exist (they perished in antiquity), and what we have are copies of copies of copies etc. of those autographs. In the absence of printing, all texts are written by hand and the only way to have several copies of a text is for each copy to be written out separately. In this process of manual copying errors of various kinds are apt to creep in: misspellings, omissions, duplications, additions, and the like.

---

[51] Law, *Historical Critical Method*, 23.

As these copies are themselves copied the likelihood of error increases. However, it is not the case that the copies that now exist come from the original autograph in the same line of descent, since the original will have been copied many times (even from the beginning) and each of these copies will then have been copied again. The result is that the copies that now survive will trace back to the original autograph by several distinct routes, and the errors that have crept in will be different in different routes. By comparing the surviving copies, it is possible to use copies from different routes of descent to correct each other and so establish a text that is closer to the original than any of them is by itself. It is also possible by application of rules of grammar or sense to correct garbled texts and restore what must have been the original form, or close to it. Textual criticism of this sort is a task for all works surviving from antiquity. It has become a highly developed art, and its worth has not seldom been confirmed by later finds of other copies or parts of copies that verify the accuracy of proposed corrections.

But as to the diachronic part proper Law distinguishes several elements. He says of what is called "source criticism" that it is concerned with identifying the sources used in the composition of biblical texts, and that it attempts to recover the building blocks from which the final text was constructed.[52] Signs typically looked for to discern these building blocks are repetitions, inconsistencies, interruptions, doublets, tensions, and variations of style. For the conflation by a later editor of different sources is posited as the most likely explanation for such features.[53] Source criticism rests on certain presuppositions, as that individual authors do not have conflicting styles, do not contradict themselves, or do not engage in disruptive tangents, so that the presence of such features in a text points to differences in author or source or the like. That these and similar

---

[52] Law, *Historical Critical Method*, 114.

[53] Law, *Historical Critical Method*, 116-118.

presuppositions are questionable is noted by Law,[54] and more will be said about them shortly.

Form criticism looks to identify and classify forms, and forms are conventional patterns of speech employed in specific contexts or in specific genres of writing. For example, the form "Dear Sir" or "Yours Sincerely" point to the genre of letter writing.[55] The setting in life or *Sitz im Leben* of a given form is the actual situation that gave rise to the form in the first place, e.g. what social, cultural, religious milieu the form arose in and was somehow a response to.[56] The form used is thus said to reflect the needs and preoccupations of the community where it arose and not vice versa; or, to put it more pointedly, the community creates the message and not the message the community.

Redaction criticism concerns how the sources, forms, settings were put together by editors, or redactors, into the final written result which is the text as we now have it (or as textual criticism has been able to provide it for us). Other accounts of these several elements differ rather in terminology and precision of detail than in substance. Gorman for instance summarizes them as follows:[57]

Textual criticism or the quest for the original wording of the text and the ways later scribes altered it.

Historical linguistics or the quest to understand the words, idioms, grammatical forms, and the relationships among these items, often with attention to their historical development within a language.

Form criticism or the quest for the original type of oral or written tradition reflected in the text, and for the sort of situation in the life of Israel or the early Church out of which such a tradition might have developed.

---

[54] Law, *Historical Critical Method*, 127, 137-139.

[55] Law, *Historical Critical Method*, 141-142; Orchard and Sutcliffe, *Catholic Commentary* §609a, p.759.

[56] Law, *Historical Critical Method*, 162-163.

[57] Michael J. Gorman in his *Elements of Biblical Exegesis: A Basic Guide for Students and Ministers* (Peabody, Mass.: Hendrickson, 2010), 16.

Tradition criticism or the quest for understanding the growth of a tradition over time from its original form to its incorporation in the final text.

Source criticism or the quest for the written and oral sources used in the text.

Redaction criticism or the quest for perceiving the ways in which the final author of the text purposefully adopted and adapted sources.

Historical criticism or the quest for the events that surrounded the production of the text, including the purported events narrated by the text itself.

The prevailing view today about the Gospels, as based on the diachronic method, is the one adopted by Meier and noted at the beginning: the Gospels belong to unknown authors dating from the late first century AD; Mark precedes Matthew and Luke and is one of their main sources along with an unknown collection of stories and sayings labeled Q, and miscellaneous collections of other material proper to each; John represents an independent tradition (as will be noted later below).

This view about the Gospels conflicts with what historical sources say about them, for these sources attribute each Gospel to the author whose names they bear (the apostles Matthew and John, Mark the follower of Peter, and Luke the follower of Paul); and they also put Matthew first in time, followed by Mark and Luke in close order, with John coming later. The diachronic method considers these historical sources to be too late and too unreliable to be believed. It holds that only literary criticism, or the use of what is gleaned through the synchronic method, can get us to the truth about the date and authorship of the Gospels. How correct this conviction is will be examined shortly.

So much then for the diachronic side of the historical critical method. As for the synchronic side, which is easier to explain and summarize, Gorman lists its parts as follows:[58]

Literary criticism or the quest to understand the text as literature by

---

[58] Gorman, *Elements of Biblical Exegesis*, 14.

employing either traditional or more recent modes of literary criticism that are common to the study of literature generally (as corollaries of literary criticism are listed genre and form analysis, or the quests to classify a text as to its type).

Narrative criticism or the quest to understand the formal and material features of narrative texts or other texts that have an implicit or underlying narrative within or behind them.

Rhetorical criticism or the quest to understand the devices, strategies, and structure employed in the text to persuade or otherwise affect the reader, as well as the overall goals or effects of those rhetorical elements.

Lexical, grammatical, and syntactical analysis or the quest to understand words, idioms, grammatical forms, and the relationships among these items according to the norms of usage at the time the text was produced.

Semantic (or discourse) analysis or the quest to understand the ways in which a text conveys meaning according to modern principles and theories of linguistics.

Social-scientific criticism is the quest for the social identity, perceptions of the world, and cultural characteristics of the writers, readers, hearers, and communities suggested by the text.

The synchronic method as so analyzed overlaps with the ancient art of rhetoric, apart from some further elaborations and developments.[59] By itself the synchronic method says nothing about historicity. It is essentially what we now call literary criticism, or the analysis of the form and structure and style of a completed text. As such the method is historically neutral, though its results can be used in arguments about historicity, for the diachronic method, as already noted, is basically the application of the results of literary criticism to the determination of historical questions.

---

[59] As rightly noted by the Catholic *Pontifical Biblical Commission*, section I.B.1

Section 3: Intrinsic Limits to Literary Criticism

The best way to show how diachronic analysis uses synchronic analysis to establish its results about who wrote what when and how is to give examples. But there is a prior and general problem about the whole diachronic approach that needs to be dealt with first, for the approach can be shown, on philosophical grounds, to be incoherent, whether as applied to the Gospels or to any other text. The argument is involved but simple enough in idea and logic. It turns on what the evidence is that is available for assessing texts, and how it may be used to draw valid conclusions about them. The essence of the argument is not new. It elaborates rather on what others have already pointed to, as in particular Leo XIII when he wrote:

> It is clear that in historical questions, such as the origin and the handing down of writings, the witness of history is of primary importance, and that historical investigations should be made with the utmost care; and that in this matter internal evidence is seldom of great value, except as confirmation.[60]

We can illustrate and strengthen Leo's warning by noting that there are, generally speaking, two basic kinds of evidence for use in arguments about authorship and dating of texts:[61] either (1) those intrinsic to the text or (2) those extrinsic to it. By the latter is meant information about the texts from other authors or from other works of the same author or from the actual material on which the original texts (or at least early copies thereof) are written. By the former is meant evidence within the texts themselves, which will be either (1.1) those based on its matter or content or (1.2) those based on its words or its verbal form. By the matter or content is meant either (1.1.1) the actual statements and arguments of the text or (1.1.2) the references present in these statements and arguments

---

[60]   Leo XIII, Encyclical, *Providentissimus Deus* (1893) §17, at the Holy See, www.vatican.va

[61]   The material that follows is adapted from what I wrote in *The Great Ethics of Aristotle,* (Routledge, 2017), xiii-xiv. Used with permission.

that go outside these statements and arguments, either to historical facts or to statements and arguments elsewhere in the same or other texts of the same or other authors. By the verbal form (1.2) is meant the style of the writing, such as its word use, its phraseology, its sentence structure, and so forth, although one should properly exclude from this division and add under 1.1.2 any verbal data, such as technical or novel or foreign vocabulary or meanings, that contain an implicit reference to external facts, say, of first invention or discovery. Arguments based on the matter one may call philosophical or theological if they regard the statements and arguments, and historical if they regard the references. Arguments based on the verbal form one may call literary and philological, or literary critical in general.

So there are four kinds of argument, one extrinsic (2) and three intrinsic, namely the philosophical or theological (1.1.1), the historical (1.1.2), and the literary critical (1.2). If one compares these kinds, it can be shown (in agreement with Leo) that no compelling argument about authenticity or dating can be made on philosophical or theological grounds alone or on literary critical grounds alone. Or, to relate the question to the present topic, no compelling diachronic arguments can be made on synchronic grounds alone. Such arguments, to be persuasive, must rely instead or additionally on extrinsic and historical grounds. The reason is as follows.

Arguments about authenticity and dating based on philosophical or theological or literary critical grounds (that is, synchronic grounds), in order to be successful, must claim that the work said to be by someone other than the alleged author contains statements or arguments or uses words or phrases or sentence structures or has organizations of material that are incompatible with the work's having the author or dating it is said to have. But in order to know that the features in question are thus incompatible, we would first need to know what works the author was or was not capable of writing when, since it is only from such knowledge that we could know that the author could not or did not write works with such features at such time. But we could only know that such author was not capable of writing such works at such time if we already knew that he did not write such works at such time. For if he did then write them, he was manifestly capable of then writing them. In other words, we would need to know that he did not then write them in order to be able to assert the premise on which the argument rests that he did not then write them. Or, we would need to know that the works were inauthentic in order to prove they were inauthentic, which is a manifest fallacy, a manifest begging of the question.

In order to make this point as clear as possible, for it may seem too quick, we can illustrate it by means of the following argumentative schemata:

1. Author A could not at time T have written any writing with properties XYZ, say theological ones (like miracles, prophecies, sophisticated religious thought) or literary critical ones (like certain words, sentences, phrases, orderings, and so forth).
2. Writing W has properties XYZ
3. Therefore author A could not have written writing W.

The problem with this argumentative schema is the first premise. For that premise must be either an empirical claim or some sort of non-empirical or a priori claim. If it is an empirical claim, it presupposes the truth of the conclusion. For we could not know that author A could not at time T write a work with properties XYZ, if we did not already know that author A did not in fact write that work at time T. For if he did then write it, which, if the claim is empirical, must at least be possible, premise 1 is false. So, to rule out this possibility and to be able to assert premise 1, we would have to know in advance that he did not then write it, which is to say we would have to know in advance that the conclusion was true, which is to beg the question. If, however, premise 1 is a non-empirical or a priori claim, it is false. There is no telling, before the event, what writings a given author could or could not write and when.

Perhaps, however, arguments about theology and style and structure are appealing for their conclusions about authorship and dating to extrinsic or historical features of the text. If so, then either these features tell us when the author could or could not write what in what way or they do not. If they do, the arguments, being extrinsic or historical, will not fall foul of the criticism. If, on the other hand, the features do not tell us when the author could or could not write what in what way, then arguments about theology and style and structure are not in fact relying on these features for their conclusions about dating and authorship but are assuming on their own what the author could or could not write when and how, which will beg the question. Or if those arguments are meant to be a priori, independent of empirical facts about what the author wrote or could write when, and to hold as matters of principle about how any author, or any such author (a first century Palestinian tax collector, for instance), could or could not write, then they will be false. There is no telling in advance how any author or any such author must write or what style or order he must use when. The human intelligence is too resourceful and the human psyche too unpredictable to be so pinned down – not to mention that in this case we also have to factor in the mysterious character of Jesus and the effect of his teaching on others, his disciples in particular.

A main objection to this reasoning is likely to be that the conclusion is altogether too strong. For even if it be true that no argument based on literary critical or synchronic criteria could show definitively that a given work was or was not by a given author at a given time, such arguments could surely show certain probabilities or likelihoods. For example, while Mark could be a sort of abbreviation of Matthew and Luke based on the oral preaching of Peter, the literary critical differences are such that they are better explained if Matthew and Luke are expansions of Mark using additional and different sources,[62] and if all three postdate the time of the apostles.

---

[62] For instance, Mark is written in less polished Greek, is shorter, and less sophisticated than Matthew and Luke. These features (to the extent they are true) would, it is said, be easy to explain if Mark was a first attempt at writing a life of Christ and if Matthew and Luke were later improvements on him, but hard to explain if Mark borrowed from Matthew or also Luke and deliberately made a worse version. Needless to say, this view falls foul of the argument being presented here. Besides, the peculiarities of Mark can be easily, or better, explained in other ways that do not put Mark first (notably the one by Orchard and Riley discussed later in chapter 5).

There are two problems with this objection. The first is that it forces us back on matters where fineness of literary judgment and skill in interpretation become dominant. Such judgment and interpretation are necessary in assessing the nature and quality of written works, but where they are relied on wholly or predominantly, the room for mistake and for the subjectivities of taste is greatly increased. Consequently decisions about dating and authenticity, instead of being based on what can be objectively or independently assessed, get based on subjective impressions or personal predilections or failure to notice different interpretative possibilities (several examples illustrating this fact will be given in the next section).

The second problem is that the objection also works the other way around. For if Luke and Matthew are expansions of Mark, or the like, and if they are not by their eponymous authors, then the extrinsic historical evidence we have that they are by their eponymous authors, and that Matthew is first and Mark and Luke next, is false. But suppose one holds, as many have and do, that the historical evidence is not false. Then Luke and Matthew cannot be expansions of Mark, nor can they all be late compositions of unknown authors, and the literary critical judgment that they are must be mistaken. Accordingly, we should look at the literary evidence again, and with much more care, to find out what is really going on. This reverse way of taking the objection differs from the initial one in that it does not accept that the literary evidence about order and dating can in fact be what it is said to be. The initial way, by contrast, does. Which way, then, is right or more reasonable? We cannot answer by appealing back to the literary evidence itself, by saying this evidence does or does not favor Markan priority and late dating, because the literary evidence is itself what is now at issue, and we cannot assume a solution to this issue without begging the question on one side or the other. So if we are going to say anything about authorship and dating, we will be forced to appeal to further and non-literary evidence (namely extrinsic historical evidence).

There is a further and related problem here as well, namely the assessment of rival hypotheses to explain the intrinsic features of given writings.

Suppose that certain writings about the same historical events (as the four Gospels, or the three Synoptics in particular) show distinctive patterns of divergence in terms of literary critical features, and further suppose that these patterns are sufficient to call for special explanation. In order to know which explanation to adopt, we would need first to consider which explanations are possible or plausible (for we need not consider outlandish possibilities, as that the authors were extra-terrestrials from some other planet).

In the case of the Gospels there are several possibilities (priority of Matthew, priority of Mark, priority of Q, and so forth). The question arises about how to decide between the truth or likelihood of these options (or of any others that might plausibly be suggested). Scholars have devoted very little attention to this question, and not surprisingly because, if we confine ourselves to literary critical matters, it has no answer. For either each of the options explains these matters or it does not. If it does not, the option is not an option but a mistake. It purports to explain but fails to do so. We must confine our attention to those options only that do explain.

Now if there is only one option left that does explain, we have sufficient reason to adopt it. But if there are more than one left (as is true in the case of the Gospels), we can have no sufficient reason, on these grounds alone, to prefer any as more true or likely than another. For *ex hypothesi* they do explain, and since explanation is the only criterion we are supposed to be using here to judge between them, all are successful. Therefore all are, to this extent, equally true or equally likely. One of these options might be simpler than another or more elegant or easier to handle or more in accord with our tastes, but it would not, on that account, be shown to be truer or more correct. The choice of one option over another, which is supposed to be a choosing of the correct or likely account over wrong or unlikely accounts, cannot, if made on literary critical grounds alone, be anything of the kind. The evidence is *ex hypothesi* not historical or extrinsic and so cannot contain any indication of facts outside the text (as time of writing or manner of transmission). But it is only by reference to such facts that we could determine, as regards options all presumed successful as explanations, which of them was more correct than which other.

This conclusion is again very strong, but it is also very limited. It concerns only one sort of evidence (literary critical or synchronic evidence) and only one set of options (those that do explain this evidence). If some of this evidence contains, whether implicitly or explicitly, extrinsic or historical data, or if some of these options turn out not to be very successful at explaining, then this conclusion will no longer apply. There will now be good reason, reason based on *further* evidence, to prefer one or more options as more correct or likely, namely those that do a better job of explaining and that better save the extrinsic or historical data. In the absence of such further data, all that a preferred scholarly explanation can do is show that the judgment about authorship and dating is compatible with such data and not that it is required by it or favored over others by it.

Section 4: Examples of the Method

In illustration of the preceding argument, and to get a clearer grasp of how the diachronic method uses literary criticism, or uses the synchronic method, to get its results (and of how perilous and arbitrary this use often is), it is best to give a few examples.

Take, then, a first example from *John* 14:31. Here, after a lengthy discourse that began in chapter 13, Jesus bids the disciples rise and depart, indicating that the discourse is over. But then the immediately following verse, the beginning of chapter 15, has Jesus continuing his discourse and doing so until the end of chapter 17. There seems to be some sort of interruption in the process of the text and a suggestion from source criticism is that John, or whoever the editor was, has slotted the material from chapter 15 into a framework provided by an earlier source and has left the join between them still visible.[63]

---

[63] Law, *Historical Critical Method*, 125, Wilhelm Egger, *How to Read the New Testament:*

If so the editorial work was not very skillful, since the join could easily have been removed by removing Jesus' command to rise and depart. Further, the idea that the command to depart is an interruption seems to betray a certain lack of literary feel, or a failure to enter into the drama of the scene. For another reading is that Jesus gives the command to depart because he sees the disciples are still not fully following him and, as the hour is late and he wants to be in the garden of Gethsemane, he gives them a temporary breather, as it were, so they can let his words sink in a bit. Then, at the beginning of chapter 15, as the disciples are walking to Gethsemane, they pass, we may suppose, a vineyard, or the topic of vineyards arises in some way, and Jesus takes advantage of it as an image to express his meaning to them better. Thus understood, the relevant phrase is not an interruption but an integral part of the discourse and the drama. There is no conflating of different traditions. There is rather the still vivid memory of a participant in the events who is recalling how the disciples did and did not understand Jesus' final discourse.

At least this alternative reading, which springs from traditional literary criticism, makes sense of the text as it stands and does not require any postulating of different sources or poor editorial work.

Another example[64] concerns peculiarities in a second passage from John. For in *John* 13:33-36, verses 34-35 interrupt the continuity between verses 33 and 36, and verses 36-38 make no reference to the new commandment introduced by verses 34-35. In addition a Greek phrase for "new commandment" in this passage occurs nowhere else in John's *Gospel* but is frequent in John's *Letters*. Moreover in those letters the command to love seems to be a command all by itself whereas in the Gospel, especially *John* 13, it has a definite content, namely keeping Jesus' words. So verses 34-35 seem, and are judged, to be a later interpolation, likely coming from the Johannine community of *1 John* which was inserted

---

An Introduction to Linguistic and Historical Critical Methodology. Trans. Peter Heinegg (Peabody, Mass.: Hendrickson, 1996), 159-161.

[64] Egger, *How to Read the New Testament*, 161-163.

into *John* 13 because *John* 13 has the type or form-genre of a "farewell address," where admonitions to love have their place.

But this example only serves to show the inadequacy of the method. The confessed aim of the method is to find marks of different layers in the text, and so a reading that promotes this aim is preferred over others. But other readings that do not support this aim lie ready to hand. Here is a possible one. The text paints the character of Peter and John. Peter, impetuous in his desire to follow Christ, is struck by Christ's saying he will go away. So he moves at once to question Christ about his going away (for the commandment does not by itself require any parting of Christ from the disciples). John, by contrast, the disciple whom Jesus loved, is struck by the commandment as much as by Peter's impetuosity. So he recalls and presents both.

Thus interpreted the text shows (in accord with ancient tradition) rather that the author of John's Gospel and of John's letters is the same than that the Gospel has been interpolated with extraneous material. The method thus seems, from this case as from others, subjective and arbitrary. It is subjective because it depends on the critic's sensitivity as a reader and on previous ideological commitments. It is arbitrary because it depends on ignoring the ancient evidence about authors and times of authorship (to be discussed in the next chapter).

Another and different example is *Matthew* 5:17 where Jesus says he has not come to abolish the law but to fulfill it. Meier asserts[65] that this verse is a creation of Matthew and his church, displaying Matthew's redactional hand. The reasons given are that the word "fulfill" is used frequently by Matthew to show how Christ fulfilled Old Testament prophecy, or how he is the eschatological fullness and consummation of the ages. The idea of fulfilment perfectly fits Matthew's theology. Indeed the statement that Christ "fulfills" the law (whereas others are said to "do, keep, or observe" the law) is unique to Matthew in the New Testament. The same goes for other phrases that Matthew puts into the mouth of Christ.

---

[65] Meier, *A Marginal Jew*, 4.41.

Meier comments[66] that the whole of *Matthew* 5:17-48 tells us much more about the theology of a Christian evangelist in the second half of the first century than it does about the teaching of a Jew named Jesus in the first half of the first century.

But it is very evident that this way of reading *Matthew* 5:17 reflects nothing in the text as such but everything in the exegetical procedure (the commitment to the historical critical method and the distinction between the historical and the theological Jesus). There is no reason on literary grounds to doubt the natural meaning of the text, namely that Jesus said what Matthew records him as saying. Of course Matthew used his own editorial or redactional intelligence to put his Gospel together, but to be an editor does not mean to be a distorter or inventor or, put more forcefully, a liar. Moreover that Matthew has a theological purpose in his Gospel (to wit an evangelical purpose in showing Jesus to be the promised Messiah) does not throw doubt on what he writes but rather confirms it: inventing words for Jesus to say is not a way of showing he is the Messiah but rather a way of showing he is not the Messiah. It is to admit that Jesus did not do what the Messiah was supposed to do and that the only way to suppose that he did is to make up stories that he did. A surer way for Matthew to undermine the purpose of his Gospel would be hard to find.

Again, in his discussion of the infancy narratives Meier[67] finds multiple features in the texts to doubt the consistency and accuracy of the reports. His main point, however, is that Matthew and Luke tell different stories, and in particular that Matthew starts with Bethlehem and has the Holy Family, after a flight to Egypt, going to Nazareth later as if neither Joseph nor Mary had been there before. Luke, by contrast, has Joseph and Mary in Nazareth and going to Bethlehem because of Augustus' decree, with no mention of a flight to Egypt. Needless to say, it is not hard to fit these two stories together in a single, coherent account (Augustine

---

[66]   Meier, *A Marginal Jew*, 4.42.

[67]   Meier, *A Marginal Jew*, 1.208-214.

already did it[68]). Moreover, the differences between the two Gospels are readily explained by their traditional origin (as related by early Church writings, to be discussed later). Matthew wrote first and primarily for the first and Jewish Christians. Hence, for instance, he begins his Gospel in the Jewish manner with an account of Jesus' genealogy back to Abraham, the great Patriarch of the Hebrews. Luke wrote later and primarily for Gentile Christians. Hence, by contrast, he makes references to Gentile figures for dating purposes, as Augustus and Tiberius, and his genealogy comes later in the Gospel and traces Jesus' descent back to Adam, the first man from whom all men arise, Jew and Gentile.

As for the Nativity stories themselves, Matthew, given his orientation, would have a concern with matters of specific Jewish interest, and the flight of the Holy Family into Egypt recalls the sojourn of the people of Israel in that country. Matthew further asserts that the Holy Family's return from Egypt after the death of Herod fulfilled the Old Testament prophecy "Out of Egypt I called my Son" (*Matthew* 2.15). Matthew thus intimates at the same time both the divinity of Jesus as Son of God, and how to read Old Testament prophecies, namely that they have a multiple meaning and refer to events both in the history of the people of Israel and in the life of the promised Messiah. Accordingly, he has no need to say anything about Mary and Joseph's prior presence in Nazareth. He need only report that they went there after the return from Egypt, for that Jesus was from Nazareth forms part of the story of his public ministry later.

Luke, by contrast, given his orientation, would have a concern with matters of specific Gentile interest, and so he would look for events in the life of Jesus that fixed them firmly in the Gentile context. So he records the census decree by Augustus and dates it by reference to the Roman governor of Syria at the time (*Luke* 2.1-5). However, he needs also to make clear what relevance the census has to Jesus, and he does so by recording the fact that Joseph and Mary had to go to Bethlehem for the census and that Jesus was born while they were there. Having thus fixed Jesus' birth

---

[68] Augustine, *De Consensu Evangelistarum*, Book 2, section 5.

by known Roman events, and being mindful that Matthew had already recorded the flight to Egypt, he has no need to mention the latter fact. Nevertheless, the previous presence of Mary and Joseph in Nazareth does explain intelligibly enough for a Gentile audience why they returned there and so why Jesus was known during his public ministry to have grown up in Nazareth. By contrast Matthew's story gives no special reason for the Holy Family, after their return from Egypt, going to Nazareth as opposed to some other town suitable for escape from Herod's successor in Judea. The reason he gives is instead another appeal to fulfilment of Jewish prophecy, mirroring the one he gave for the original flight to Egypt (*Matthew* 2.23). Both his and Luke's explanations are correct, of course, but in different ways and at different levels. For each answers to a different purpose according to the different purposes and audiences that the historical evidence (if we take it seriously) tells us the two Gospels have.

The point may be confirmed by the fact that Matthew records the visit of the Magi and the jealous reaction of Herod (*Matthew* 2.1-18), while Luke records the story of the shepherds and the angels (*Luke* 2.8-18). Matthew's story enables him, as Luke's story would not, to show again the fulfilment of Jewish prophecies (the birth of the Messiah in Bethlehem and the murder of the children). Luke omits the story of the Magi and Herod, no doubt in part because Matthew had already recorded it, but also perhaps because a Gentile audience would likely be less impressed by fulfilment of ancient prophecies from the Old Testament than by fulfilment of contemporary divine messages. After all, Gentiles were perfectly familiar with visitations by spiritual beings and the fulfilment of these beings' predictions, since their poetry and histories and religious practice were full of both. So Luke records the angelic messages to Zechariah (*Luke* 1.11-22, 59-66), Mary (*Luke* 1.26-38), and the shepherds, and how they were soon realized. He does also, of course, record fulfilment of prophecy (e.g. *Luke* 3.1-6), and Matthew records angelic appearances (*Matthew* 1.20-21, 2.19-20). But again Matthew associates these appearances with fulfilment of Jewish prophecy, and Luke puts the fulfilled prophecy in the context of Gentile dating and notes (unlike *Matthew* 3.3) its extension to "all people."

More no doubt could be said and elaborated along the same general lines, but what is striking is how Meier makes no mention of any such ways of understanding and contextualizing the nativity stories. Instead, he sticks to his rejection of the relevant historical evidence about the origin of the Gospels, and ends up, so to say, tilting at windmills or, to put it more appositely, straining at gnats and swallowing camels. He cannot, after all, deny that there are ways of reading the texts, ways perfectly consistent with the principles and practices of literary criticism (not to say with the historical tradition about the writing of the Gospels), that involve no inconsistencies or contradictions or tensions. Meier may not like such interpretations but, since they are possible, to reject them for interpretations that are incoherent or inconsistent is not to show that the texts are incoherent or inconsistent but rather to show that one prefers incoherent and inconsistent interpretations. "Chacun à son goût," one is inclined to say, but to put forward one's "goût" as an exercise in, or the result of, careful research and sound literary scholarship is not just absurd but offensive. It is to replace study with prejudice, argument with verbal fiat, and learning with embrace of a partisan agenda.

A final and more involved, as well as more interesting case of partisan literary criticism, comes from Law on *Matthew* 15:21-28 and *Mark* 7:24-30, about the cure of a Gentile woman's daughter.[69] Law identifies in Matthew several forms, as that of miracle story, of controversy dialogue, and of pronouncement story, which is fair enough if these forms are taken simply to be elements within the whole episode. But Law thinks that the episode has been conflated by Matthew from forms that originally existed in separation.

Such a supposition is not impossible, of course, but it is neither necessary nor convincing as literary criticism. The story in both texts presents itself rather as a whole unit recording an actual event in Jesus'

---

[69]   Law, *Historical Critical Method*, 175

ministry. Scholars, however, use the supposition of conflation from different forms to conclude that the whole episode is the reflection back into the life of Jesus of post-Easter debates concerning the status of Gentiles in the Church. They further suppose that because of the hostility toward the Gentile woman on Christ's part that the story seems to display, it must have originated in a Palestinian context and not in Gentile Christianity. For, they say, a text originating among Gentile Christians would show Jesus to be unequivocally supportive of the Gentile mission rather than display the reluctant and ambiguous response described by Matthew.[70]

Now this supposition not only assumes the original dissolution of the passage into separate forms (as opposed to the forms being an integral literary whole), but also assumes the diachronic method's concern to use such dissolution to draw historical conclusions. The failure of the method here is sufficiently shown by the external historical facts. For Mark has the same story, save without Matthew's alleged ambiguity, and Luke does not have it at all. The difference between Matthew on the one hand and Mark and Luke on the other can be sufficiently explained by what historical evidence tells us, namely that Matthew was written first and for a predominantly Jewish audience; that Mark was a sort of epitome of Matthew (and to a lesser extent of Luke) based on Peter's teaching, especially in Rome; and that Luke was written, under the prompting of St. Paul, predominantly for Gentiles.

These historical facts support the *Sitz im Leben* that we get from the history of *Acts*, that the early Church did have some difficulty accepting that the Gospel was meant for Gentiles and not just for Jews, as in the episode about Peter and Cornelius, *Acts* 10-11. But the acceptance came quickly enough, as that episode itself shows, despite some lingering opposition (*Galatians* 1-2). So, one would expect Matthew to pay attention, as he does throughout, to things of special concern to Jews, while one would expect Luke to do so less (or only to do so insofar as Jewish things were integral to the Gospel message, as the stories about the births of John the

---

[70] Law, *Historical Critical Method*, 175, 209-210.

Baptist and Jesus). One would also expect Mark, in an epitome, to omit details found in Matthew, and one would further expect these omitted details to include perplexities peculiar to preceding Jewish tradition that the Church had resolved (save for some recalcitrant hold-outs), and that were not of concern to Peter's immediate audience.

Nevertheless there is nothing in Matthew that conflicts with the Church's later resolution or indeed with Jesus' actual words and deeds, contrary to what the diachronic method wants.[71] For if Matthew's record-ing of the story is read with some subtlety of literary sense, it can be seen that Jesus' discussion with the Gentile woman is meant precisely to teach the Apostles, and so through them the Church they were to found, that Gentiles are to be fully part of the Church. The very fact that the Gentile woman has so great faith and thereby wins her desired miracle from Jesus shows, above all to the Apostles, that faith can be found as much among the Gentiles as the Jews, and that Jesus intends his Church and its salvific benefits to be for Gentiles as well as Jews. But because Jesus bestows sal-vation and founds a Church in virtue of being the promised Messiah, and because the idea and prophecy of the Messiah was given to and through the Jews alone and not the Gentiles, Jesus' mission and his Church cannot be understood, even by Gentiles, without the Jewish origin.

In this sense indeed, Jesus was sent only to the Jews (as Matthew records), for only the Jews had the necessary preparation, the Law and the Prophets, to be able to understand who Jesus was. But being thus sent only *to* the Jews is not the same as, nor does it entail, being sent only *for* the Jews. Indeed, this very story of the Gentile woman proves that Jesus was not sent only *for* the Jews. The woman's remarkable persistence and faith (which Jesus may be understood as deliberately and providentially provoking), and Jesus' performing the miracle for her, prove that when Jesus says he was sent to the Jews, the meaning is not (as the Apostles and many Jews were inclined initially to think) that the Messiah was sent only *for* the Jews. It can only mean that the Messiah is only *of* or *from* or

---

[71] Law, *Historical Critical Method*, 209-210.

through the Jews but that he is *for* everyone, including the Gentiles. The story, in fact, while about a Gentile is chiefly of benefit to the Jews, so that the Jews, and the Apostles in particular, will not let popular but false Jewish opinions prevent them from seeing what the true mission of the Messiah is. For that mission cannot be understood even by the Apostles if it is not understood to be in its goal, though not in its origin, as much Gentile as Jewish.

Mark's omission, therefore, of Matthew's details should not be read as a sign that Matthew is later and reflects subsequent conflicts between Jewish and Gentile Christians and not what Jesus actually said and did. To suppose so is without sufficient warrant even on literary grounds, let alone historical ones. The words of Jesus recorded by Matthew do not reflect such conflicts but anticipate and resolve them, however slow some in the early Church were to appreciate the fact. These conflicts, as the episode with Peter and Cornelius makes clear, had anyway long been declared misconceived and it was Jewish Christians who were trying to reignite them. Paul's rebuke of Peter (*Galatians* 2-11-14) when Peter was acting otherwise proves the fact, for Paul merely repeats what Peter must, in his heart of hearts, have known from his experience with Cornelius. Accordingly, Luke's omission of the story of the Gentile woman is not a sign that the story is a later invention reflecting a *Sitz im Leben* that was different from that in which Matthew wrote. Rather it is a sign that Luke, who as we know from historical evidence was writing for Gentile audiences, chose not to include a miracle story whose details, however factually true, would not aid such audiences, or not aid them as much as other miracle stories would that were no less factually true but were more fitted to his purpose.

Yet, despite these differences in purpose, the Gospels can be as historically true as one could want. In this respect they are comparable, as history and as writings, with other biographies and histories, as those of Plutarch, Sallust, Suetonius, Thucydides, or Xenophon. For these authors too selected and presented genuinely historical material according to a definite intention and method.[72] We can, then, use the idea of difference of purpose to explain the differences between the Gospels, as in particular their treatment of the Gentile question. But here the historical evidence about the origin of the several Gospels is of especial importance, since it gives us firm extrinsic support for what the internal literary evidence, fairly weighed, already itself supports. Certainly we have no basis to use, or rather misuse, the internal literary evidence to construct theories of origin or *Sitze im Leben* that not only ignore the historical evidence but directly conflict with it. Honesty to the principles of historical research and to truth forbids us so to proceed, that is, forbids us to do what devotees of the historical critical method regularly do.

From all the above we may conclude that the diachronic method is, first, just the synchronic method, or standard literary criticism, applied to questions of truth, authorship, and dating, and second that such application, as actually carried out, is fallacious. The method as in fact followed by Biblical critics depends on philosophical, theological, and historical assumptions that have neither fact nor reason nor literary sense behind them. No Gospel passages appealed to by critics to show that the Gospels are mutually incoherent, or to show the priority of Mark, are incapable of being interpreted as well, or better, to show their mutual harmony and the priority of Matthew. The examples given above are enough to make the point but many more could be given to the same effect. It suffices to read Augustine or the several comprehensive lives of Christ to appreciate the fact.[73]

---

[72] That the Gospels fall within the ancient literary genre of biographies, or historical lives, has been well argued by Richard A. Burridge, *What are the Gospels? A Comparison with Greco-Roman Biography* (Grand Rapids: Wm. B. Eerdmans Publishing, 2004).

[73] Augustine *De Consensu*, Giuseppe Ricciotti, *Life of Christ* (Milwaukee: Bruce, 1947), L.C. Fillion, *Life of Christ* (London: Herder, 1929).

CHAPTER 4

EXTERNAL HISTORICAL EVIDENCE

Section 1: Matters of Principle

What then about the extrinsic and historical evidence for the dating and authorship of the Gospels since, as noted, rejection of the ancient evidence is integral to the historical critical method? Indeed, if this evidence were accepted, while there would still be questions about the artistry or literary critical elements of the Gospels (of the sort that scholars and theologians have long discussed and answered in different ways), there would be none about how these elements are to be mined for constructing theories about dating and authorship. The ancient evidence would already have answered such questions, at least as to the basic fact if not as to all the details.

The rejection of the ancient evidence is curious, and first because it is comparatively recent. Up until about the 1600s this evidence was considered to be decisive. What happened or changed for the view of the ancient evidence to change? The short answer is the rationalism that led to the rejection of the supernatural, as is evident particularly in Spinoza.[74] The original rationalism of Spinoza has long since been dismissed, but

---

[74] In his *Tractatus Theologico-Politicus*, 1670. http://spinozaetnous.org/wiki/Tractatus_ theologico-politicus

the rejection of the supernatural, and the limitation, or rather reduction, of the natural to the materially scientific has remained. The limitation has no warrant.

There is no good reason to suppose that the material or natural sciences are adequate to the whole of experienced reality, or to suppose that, because the natural sciences do not concern themselves with what transcends natural causes, therefore the supernatural does not exist. The limits of these sciences are built into their method and are legitimate as far as they go. What is not legitimate is to make merely methodological posits into an ontological principle. To do so has no justification in fact or reason. Not in reason because whether there is anything supernatural in the world is a matter of empirical evidence, and reason must follow the evidence not rule some of it out a priori. Not in fact because there is plenty of empirical evidence of supernatural things happening both now and in the past.[75] Such evidence needs to be weighed carefully, of course, but whether the evidence stands up to examination is something that presupposes the collection of the evidence, and one cannot, without begging the question, reject some of the evidence from the collection because it does not fit the theory one prefers. The theory must be determined by the evidence, not the evidence by the theory. On this point Leo XIII was again percipient:

> higher criticism will resolve itself into the reflection of the bias and the prejudice of the critics... and seeing that most of them are tainted with false philosophy and rationalism, it must lead to the elimination from the sacred writings of all prophecy and miracle, and of everything else that is outside the natural order.[76]

In support of this argument, and to confirm the oddity of the attitude taken toward the historical evidence by practitioners of the historical

---

[75] Miracles and exorcisms are the most obvious, perhaps, and both are well attested. Some discussion in Meier, *A Marginal Jew*, 2.528 n20.

[76] *Providentissimus Deus*, §17.

critical method, it is worth quoting some of their more telling remarks. Take, then, an example from Orchard and Riley who thus cite Raymond Brown.

> Nor is the appeal to tradition satisfactory, for in questions of authorship the Church writers simply copied each other (or expanded what they received with legendary additions). Most of the time the "tradition" about such an issue, however unanimous, has little more value than the credibility of the first attestation.[77]

"Quod gratis asseritur gratis negatur," as the Latin tag has it ("what is gratuitously asserted is gratuitously denied"). How does Brown know that the sources copied each other or added legend to tradition? Further, how does he know that the tradition begins with a first attestation rather than with multiple attestations, both oral and written, from multiple eyewitnesses? And even if the tradition does begin with one first attestation, if that attestation was correct (and what reason is there to think it was not?), the whole tradition is correct. Besides, if the first witness was not correct, others would soon have corrected him, for assuredly many knew even if many did not write it down. Written witnesses would thus be quoting many sources and not some supposed single first source. Further, Brown and all modern scholars postdate the events by some 2,000 years while the historical sources referred to postdate the events by little more than a hundred. If the latter are not to be trusted despite their closeness to the events and their access to other sources now lost, even more are modern scholars not to be trusted because of their greater distance and lack of access to such sources.[78]

---

[77] Raymond Brown, *The Critical Meaning of the Bible* (Chapman: London 1981). Cited by Orchard and Riley, *The Order of the Synoptics*, 114n.

[78] Note incidentally that support for the early authority and pre-eminence of Matthew's Gospel is found in the many implicit citations from it in early Christian writers, while there are none from Mark and few from Luke, which is hardly compatible with Markan priority, as is aptly remarked by Orchard and Riley, *The Order of the Synoptics*, 120-121.

In contrast to Brown, take a couple of other quotes:

> The important point to be noticed is the easy way in which the savants of the age separated themselves from the historical evidence provided by the documents of early Christian literature. On the whole it must be said that both in its origins and its later development higher criticism has signally failed in respect for external historical evidence about the composition of the Gospels. Right from the beginning it put its trust in its power of literary analysis rather than in the broader approach which includes analysis and historical tradition alike... To find the right answer in matters such as this a shred of external evidence is more valuable than all speculations built upon internal evidence alone.[79]

Note here the remark of Vincent Taylor that "if the Form critics are right the disciples must have been translated to heaven immediately after the Resurrection."[80] Taylor's point is that the disciples, or several of them, lived to the time of Nero and beyond, and would consequently have been in a perfect position to correct, by direct personal experience, deviations from what they themselves knew to be true.

Consider too the treatment by modern scholars of the *Ecclesiastical History* of Eusebius (260-340AD), which is one of our main sources of evidence for the dating and authorship of the Gospels. It preserves for us information not found elsewhere. There is, of course, no trace in Eusebius of modern theories about dating and authorship, which are a very recent product. It behooves modern writers, therefore, not to impugn Eusebius on the grounds that his writing is late (some 200 years from the end of the

---

[79] Orchard and Sutcliffe, *Catholic Commentary*, §§604e, 607e, pp.753, 756. See also A. Camerlynck and H. Coppieters, *Synopsis Evangeliorum* (Bruges: Beyaert Publ., 1910), xxxv: "Argumentum externum...multo majoris est ponderis quam rationes internae." "External evidence is of much greater weight than internal reasons."

[80] Vincent Taylor, *The Formation of the Gospel Tradition* (London: Macmillan, 1957) 41.

Apostolic age and over 250 from the time of Jesus). The writings of modern scholars are much later. Besides Eusebius had access to documents that are lost to us. It is presumptuous on our part to dismiss his citations and references, since he knew what he was talking about and we do not. Further, if Eusebius got things wrong, or even was deliberately deceitful, contemporaries (who again had access to information we do not) would have been quick to point it out. Indeed the Church historian Socrates (ca. 380-439) did think Eusebius was unreliable in certain respects,[81] but these respects concerned contemporary events about the Emperor Constantine I and not about the Gospels, and notably Socrates did not choose to impugn or correct what Eusebius said about them.

Indeed, if we compare the way Eusebius used the documents available to him with the way modern scholars use the documents available to them (the Gospels themselves, the very *History* of Eusebius, and numerous others mentioned below), we will find Eusebius a more reliable writer. He does not dismiss or wrest his documents in the way modern scholars dismiss and wrest theirs, for the latter dismiss all the ancient evidence about authorship and dating, and wrest the data of the Gospels in all kinds of historical-critical ways so as to support their theories.

Their rejection, for instance, of the reality of the miracles and prophecies and exorcisms of demons with which the Gospels abound is not historically based. It is based, as already remarked, on so-called rationalist views about the non-existence of a divine power that would intervene in history to cause such things. But one certainly cannot conclude on empirical grounds that there is no such power, for miracles, if they happen, are part of those grounds. So whether any miracles have happened or not must first be empirically established in order then to conclude whether any power exists that would intervene miraculously in history to cause them. Ruling out such a power, and against the empirical witness of the Gospels too, is thus not done on empirical grounds. It is done on a priori

---

[81] Socrates, *Church History* 1.1, 10, at http://www.newadvent.org/fathers/26011.htm The fact, however, is admitted, in a way, by Eusebius himself, *Church History*, 8.2, at http://www.newadvent.org/fathers/2501.htm

philosophical grounds, or rather on grounds of ideological prejudice, and these grounds are then used to reject or explain away the Gospel data. Eusebius did not proceed thus in his history but followed the empirical record itself. So, if we must trust modern scholars or Eusebius for our knowledge and understanding of the Gospels, we should trust Eusebius and not them.

Now the important point about Eusebius as regards the Gospels is that he repeats and confirms the tradition as we know it from other and earlier writers (as will be summarized shortly). An important and careful examination of Eusebius, as of much else to do with the authorship and dating of the Gospels, is found in the book by Orchard and Riley (to be discussed more below),[82] where a thorough review of all the evidence is given, and where, more importantly, a thorough review of Eusebius is given too. The upshot is that the external evidence for the tradition about the Gospels (Matthew first, Mark and Luke close second and third, John fourth) is solid, unanimous, and historically unimpeachable. It can fairly be said that, on the basis of the external evidence, the supposition of Markan priority was exploded before, during, and after its invention. If scholars still cling to Markan priority (as many do), the reason cannot be anything historical, for history is solidly against such priority. It can only be literary and theological, or the view that the internal form and content of Mark in comparison with Matthew and Luke are such that Mark must be first. The trouble, however, with such appeals to internal form and content, as has been argued above, is, first, that they are circular (they assume what they want to prove), and, second, highly contestable.

The internal evidence can be accounted for in many ways, and some of these ways are perfectly compatible with the traditional dating and authorship of the Gospels (as has been shown above). These other ways make as good or better sense of the internal evidence. But whether they do so or not, they are certainly successful, and since they are, no case is left for rejecting the external and historical evidence.

---

[82] Orchard and Riley, *The Order of the Synoptics*. Orchard and Sutcliffe's *Catholic Commentary* also records this data in its introduction to each of the Gospels.

It is a principle of sound method, and certainly of a sound historical method, to give an account that saves all or most of the evidence. But the modern accounts based on Markan priority save none of the external and historical evidence; rather they openly reject it. To call such a method historical is bizarre. It is just as bizarre to call it critical, for it displays hardly any *crisis* or *judgment* at all. In fact what it displays is *pre-judgment*, or as we say *pre-judice*, because it does not judge the Gospels on the basis of the evidence but on the basis of philosophical or ideological convictions that are formed and adopted prior to and indeed against the evidence. The fact is plain from the rejection of miracles and other supernatural phenomena that one finds in the Gospels. For to come to the Gospels with the supposition that supernatural phenomena are historically impossible, or impossible for a historian as historian to accept, is to come to the Gospels having pre-supposed that they are not historical memoirs by eyewitnesses, or by eyewitnesses of eyewitnesses, but mixtures of half-forgotten stories, mythical additions, ex post facto projections, and self-serving propaganda. If such a procedure is not pre-judice, it is hard to see what is.

The science of history, properly considered, requires us to follow the empirical evidence and not interpret the text in ways that conflict with it. Even if such interpretations are possible and can, with cleverness, be made to sound plausible, they are nevertheless to be rejected in favor of other interpretations that are compatible both with the literary features of the text and with the historical evidence. Such interpretations certainly exist and can be found already in St. Augustine as well as still in contemporary scholars. There is no reason to reject these interpretations. Indeed there is every reason to accept them, since they save all the data, historical and literary. If some scholars prefer other interpretations that, though compatible with the literary features of the text, are nevertheless incompatible with the historical evidence, then so much the worse for those scholars. Sound method counsels interpretations that save all the data, not others that save only some and conflict with the rest, especially when these others require one to attribute ignorance or naivety or deceit to the redactors.

Section 2: Summary of the Gospel Evidence

The historical evidence for the authenticity and authorship of the Gospels has been summarized by many authors. The *Catholic Commentary* mentions, in order: Papias (in Eusebius), Irenaeus, Justin, the Old Latin Prologues, the Muratorian Canon, Tertullian, Clement, Origen, Tatian.[83] Orchard and Riley deal with the same sources at greater length, but they begin with very early writings where particular Gospels are not named but where the influence in particular of Matthew, including verbal echoes, is very marked.[84] The first evidence they give is from St. Paul who in 1 and 2 *Thessalonians* (dated no later than 51-52 AD) is almost certainly referencing Matthew's Gospel, for the thought and verbal echoes are telling. So in *Matthew* 23-25 (Christ's eschatological teaching) and in the eschatological sections of 1and 2 *Thessalonians* we find the same teaching, the same metaphors and similes, and the same key words, some of them very rare.[85] If Paul is not directly citing, he is directly echoing, so much so that the echoes are as sufficient a sign of dependence as echoes of Homer, say, would be in Virgil or other poets. The like echoes can be found in Christian writings before Irenaeus (ca. 115-180). Indeed in all citations in the Church Fathers from the Gospels, Matthew is referenced the most. Luke comes a distant second and Mark seldom. This fact gives support to the view that Matthew was first, enjoying pre-eminence as the Gospel that people most and first went to for facts about Jesus' life and teaching.[86]

A further piece of evidence relative to Luke and Luke's Gospel as oriented primarily to Gentiles comes in recent scholarship on Josephus (37-c.100AD) and the famous Testimonium Flavianum in his *Antiquities of the Jews*.[87] Josephus' *Antiquities*, like Luke's *Gospel*, is a work about

---

[83]   Orchard and Sutcliffe, *Catholic Commentary*, §606b, p754.

[84]   Orchard and Riley, *The Order of the Synoptics*, 118-122

[85]   Orchard and Riley, *The Order of the Synoptics*, 119-120

[86]   Orchard and Riley, *The Order of the Synoptics*, 122.

[87]   Josephus, *Antiquities of the Jews* 18.3.3.

Jewish matters directed to a Gentile audience. The authenticity of the Testimonium has been disputed.[88] An intriguing article, however, which also defends it, has pointed out that the whole Testimonium as actually written echoes a passage in Luke's *Gospel* about the two disciples on the road to Emmaus.[89]

The passage in Luke reads as follows (Lk 24:19-27):

...the things about Jesus the Nazarene, who was a prophet mighty in deed and word before God and all the people, and how our chief priests and leaders handed him over to the judgment of death and crucified him. But we had hoped that he was the one to redeem Israel... it is now the third day since these things took place. Moreover, some women of our group...were at the tomb early this morning...they came back and told us that they had... seen a vision of angels who said that he was alive... Then he said to them, "... Was it not necessary that the Messiah should suffer these things and then enter into his glory?" Then beginning with Moses and all the prophets, he interpreted to them the things about himself in all the scriptures.

The Passage in Josephus reads:

About this time there was Jesus, a wise man, if indeed one ought to call him a man. For he was one who performed surprising deeds and was a teacher of such people as accept the truth gladly... He was the Christ. And when, upon an accusation by the principal men among us, Pilate had condemned him to a cross, those who had in the first place come to love him did not

---

[88]   Meier, *A Marginal Jew*, 1.61-69. Meier's discussion of this passage is more moderate than many but he still objects to parts of it as spurious.

[89]   Gary J. Goldberg, 'The Coincidences of the Emmaus Narrative of Luke and the Testimonium of Josephus,' *the Journal for the Study of the Pseudepigrapha* 13 (1995) 59-77. The translations in the text are taken from Goldberg.

give up their affection for him. He appeared to them spending a third day restored to life, for the prophets of God had prophesied these things and countless other marvels about him.[90]

The parallels here are intriguing enough, as Goldberg explains, especially by comparisons of the original Greek and the actual words used in both passages, to suggest that Josephus was adapting Luke, or perhaps a source common to himself and Luke (which must ultimately be the two disciples themselves). If so, Josephus is our first non-Christian evidence of the Gospel tradition. The point should not be pressed perhaps, but neither should it be ignored.

Papias (ca. 60-134/8) is the first we know of who mentions the four Gospel authors by name, but we lack his original works and have only citations in Eusebius. These citations should be enough, nevertheless, to inform us about what Papias said, though modern scholars throw the same cloud over his words as over Eusebius who cites them.

Otherwise there are no surviving mentions of the names of the authors of the Gospel prior to about 150AD, but a sufficient reason is that up until then the tradition was in tranquil possession and hardly needed to be mentioned (for all knew it and accepted it). Around that time, however, the heresy of Marcion (ca. 80-160) had developed and become widespread, and Marcion explicitly rejected the fourfold Gospel, retaining only a shortened version of Luke. At that point, then, there was express need for the Church and Church writers to insist on the four Gospels and their Apostolic origin. The evidence of Justin (ca.100-165) confirms the fact, for while he speaks freely of the "memoirs" of the Apostles, he does not bother to name them.[91] He had after all no need to do so, since the fact the Gospels were memoirs of definitely known Apostles was itself well known and without serious challenge (Mark and Luke, though not themselves Apostles, were known to be followers of the

---

[90] Josephus, *Antiquities* 18.3.3.

[91] Justin, *First Apology* 66.

Apostles Peter and Paul). There is nevertheless one passage where Justin seems to refer expressly to the memoirs of Peter and quotes from Mark.[92] Not to be ignored here is Justin's pupil Tatian, who wrote a harmony of the four Gospels or his so-called *Diatessaron* (ca. 150-180). The work survives now mainly in quotations in Syriac from a commentary on it by Ephrem the Syrian (306-373), though a Latin version, rather altered in line with the Vulgate, still survives.[93] In any event its very existence shows the credit the four canonical Gospels enjoyed in Justin's day as the memoirs of the Apostles.

The first explicit reference to the authorship and dating of the four Gospels in an author whose texts we still have is Irenaeus (ca. 115-180), *Adv.Haer.* III.1.1. Irenaeus tells us the following. Matthew the Apostle is first and written during the lifetimes of Peter and Paul (both of whom were martyred between 66-68BC); Mark is second as companion and recorder of the teaching of Peter; Luke is third as companion and follower of Paul (so these Gospels too, at least in their origin if not also in their publication, precede 66-68BC); and John the Apostle is last and fourth, but Irenaeus does not say how much later.[94] Clement of Alexandria (ca.150-215) gives the same account for Mark and Luke. He and Tertullian (ca. 155-220) and Origen (ca. 185-253) all record the same order and authorship for the Gospels, as does the Muratorian canon and the old Latin or Anti-Marcionite prologues to the Gospels. The dating of the Muratorian canon and of the Latin prologues is disputed but seems to be mid to late second century.[95] Their importance, even independently of dating, is that they repeat the same story about the Gospels. There is not a trace anywhere in these sources of the opinion of modern scholars that Mark is

---

[92] *Dial. Trypho* 106.9-10, Orchard and Riley, *The Order of the Synoptics*, 125.

[93] William J. Petersen, 'Textual Evidence of Tatian's Dependence on Justin's Apomnemoneumata', *New Testament Studies* 36 (1990): 512-534.

[94] For a fuller discussion about the dating of John see chapter 6 below.

[95] Orchard and Riley, *The Order of the Synoptics*, 138-139, 143.

first, or that the Gospels are not by the persons whose names they bear, or that they are of much later date (post 70AD).

The same listing of historical sources, and endorsement of them, are found in other writings, especially those that precede the dominance of the historical critical method. A fine instance is T. H. Horne who writes (1861) in general terms as follows:

> The books of the New Testament are quoted or alluded to by a series of Christian writers as well as by adversaries of the Christian faith, who may be traced back in regular succession from the present time to the apostolic age.[96]

He then continues to list quotations from Christian writers backwards from the fourth century, noting that the works of Christian writers from the fourth century and later are

> ...so full of references to the New Testament that it becomes unnecessary to adduce their testimonies, especially as they would only prove that the books of Scripture never lost their character or authority with the Christian Church.

He proceeds also to give comment on these writers, but his discussion and list are so extensive that the material is best relegated to an Appendix.

The well-foundedness of the traditional attributions of the Gospels is fully supported by the great and first historian of the early Church, Eusebius. There is, to be true, some dispute about John, for Eusebius says there were two Johns, one the Apostle and the other the so-called Presbyter and, while attributing the Gospel to the former, he attributed the Apocalypse to the latter. But Orchard and Riley argue convincingly that Eusebius is misreading his quotation from Papias when he thus distinguishes two Johns. Anyway Eusebius' musings would concern only the

---

[96]   Horne, *Summary of the Evidence*, 69

Apocalypse, and not the Gospels either of John or of the other three, whose early dating as well as authenticity and authorship he fully endorses.

On the basis, then, of this review of the evidence, and if we are to follow the principles of historical science and determine empirical facts (as about who wrote what when) by empirical evidence, we are bound to conclude that the Gospels are by the apostles or the men of the Apostolic age whose names they bear, and that Matthew is first. No other opinion can count as historically grounded or as compatible with the principles of history.

CHAPTER 5

HISTORICAL ANSWERS

Section 1: Church Documents

The position of the Churches on the historical critical method and on questions of Scriptural analysis has been made reasonably clear, at least in the case of the Catholic Church, in several official documents. This position was largely endorsed by the Protestant Churches too, at least at the beginning and in general terms if not in all details.[97] Accordingly the teaching of the Catholic documents can be taken as representative of traditional Protestant teaching as well. The first such document (already cited above) is *Providentissimus Deus* of Leo XIII published in 1893 when the historical critical method was waxing strong, especially among Protestant exegetes, and challenging the hitherto prevailing consensus. Leo did not condemn Biblical research or literary criticism, but he did warn against the rationalism of the historical critical method, and against using literary criticism as a way to settle historical questions in preference

---

[97] Protestant Churches accept the same Gospels as the Catholic Church, of course (as well as the rest of the New Testament canon) and, at least at the beginning, fully endorsed their authenticity and historicity. The differences between the Catholic and Protestant traditions concern rather the Old Testament, where the so-called deutero-canonical books are accepted as canonical by Catholics but generally not by Protestants (though they are regarded by the latter with respect). These differences are not germane to the present study, which is about the Gospels only.

to, or even against, the historical evidence. As he expressly said in passages already cited above:

> It is clear that in historical questions, such as the origin and the handing down of writings, the witness of history is of primary importance, and that historical investigations should be made with the utmost care; and that in this matter internal evidence is seldom of great value, except as confirmation... [H]igher criticism will resolve itself into the reflection of the bias and the prejudice of the critics... and seeing that most of them are tainted with false philosophy and rationalism, it must lead to the elimination from the sacred writings of all prophecy and miracle, and of everything else that is outside the natural order. [98]

These words of Leo were backed up and applied in a number of decisions handed down by the Pontifical Biblical Commission in succeeding years. So, for instance, the Commission confirms that Matthew's Gospel was written by Matthew, that it preceded the other Gospels, that it was written before 70AD, that it is historically accurate and reliable. It confirms that the Gospels of Luke and Mark are by Mark the disciple of Peter and Luke the disciple of Paul, that they are historically reliable, that they were composed before 70AD. On the other hand, it allows, subject to the above determinations, freedom to exegetes to discuss and hypothesize about the mutual relations between and dependence of the first three, or Synoptic, Gospels. [99]

The encyclical *Divino Afflante Spiritu*[100] of Pius XII, published in 1943 to commemorate the 50th anniversary of *Providentissimus Deus*, is no different in its teaching. For although the encyclical has been claimed

---

[98] *Providentissimus Deus*, §17.

[99] These decisions come from the years 1911 and 1912. Full references and English translation can be found at http://www.catholicapologetics.info/scripture/oldtestament/commission.htm

[100] Pius XII, Encyclical, *Divino Afflante Spiritu* (1943). At www.vatican.va

as giving encouragement to the historical critical method and thereby to "Biblical progress," the document hardly does anything of the kind. What it encourages, when properly considered, is rather what scholars had already been doing, namely careful study of the Biblical text, of the manner of writing of the ancient authors, of new material discoveries in archaeology, of textual criticism in light of newly discovered manuscripts, and the like. It emphatically repeats, in line with millennia long tradition, the teaching about the inerrancy and historical accuracy of the Biblical text. It allows, indeed encourages, use of other sciences for the study of Scripture but never endorses, nor gives any color of endorsing, the dissolving acid, so to say, of historical critical analysis such as one finds in many studies of the so-called synoptic problem.

When we come to Vatican II we find the same in *Dei Verbum*, or the dogmatic constitution on divine revelation, approved by Paul VI in 1965.[101] The document follows Pius XII's *Divino Afflante* in asserting that Scripture must be read according to both its human instrument and its divine intention, and that the particular historical facts of culture and modes of writing of the human authors must be carefully noted, but within the context of Scripture as a whole and the tradition of the Church. It says that the Gospels in particular are historically accurate records of the life of Christ and that, with due regard to the particular purposes of each Gospel writer, they tell us the honest truth about Jesus. There is straight continuity here with *Divino Afflante* and thereby also with *Providentissimus Deus*.

The only change in more recent documents is that express cognizance is taken of the historical critical method, in large part, one supposes, because of the many Catholic scholars who had followed their Protestant counterparts in adopting that method and endorsing its claims. Thus, *The Interpretation of the Bible in the Church* by the Pontifical Bible Commission in 1994[102] expressly notes, in line with tradition, that the Bible is a writing

---

[101] Paul VI, Dogmatic Constitution, *Dei Verbum* (1965). At www.vatican.va

[102] Pontifical Biblical Commission, *The Interpretation of the Bible in the Church*.

both divine and human, and that it must be examined in both respects. In chapter 1 the commission discusses the historical-critical method, whose germ it finds already present in Jerome and Origen. It details the diachronic and synchronic elements and allows that the method marks an advance in scientific and objective analysis, but only if it is not marred, as it should not be, by prejudice or a priori posits. Hermeneutics too, with its idea that understanding always involves a pre-understanding coloring how the text is appropriated, is allowed, but with a warning against so historicizing everything that the eternal and divine dimension, and the universal, trans-historical significance of Christ, are lost. There is, after all, as argued above in the first chapter, a necessary existential orientation and historical context to all human thinking, but this orientation and context are universal and the same everywhere, being focused as they are on the fundamental questions of the human condition as such. History, properly understood, supports this universality and does not undermine it.

The "pre-understanding" anyway of Biblical exegesis is the living tradition of the Church and of believers. going back to the beginning. This tradition, found more or less in many if not all Christian persuasions, holds the canon to be divinely inspired and to possess, in true existential fashion, a unique salvific and theological significance. This tradition is open-minded to a plurality of methods applied to Scripture study but is not naïve about their limits and assumptions. Diachronic methods, therefore, are insufficient without synchronic ones, and the synchronic ones, by the very idea of what it means to be synchronic, require fidelity to tradition. Similar views were endorsed by Benedict XVI in his *Verbum Domini* of 2010.[103] Benedict also begins with the existential context of all human understanding, namely in this case man's need for and the fact of salvation (which is the "pre-understanding," explicitly or implicitly, of all human thinking and acting). The document stresses that the history of salvation is true history and not myth, that it should be studied

---

[103] Benedict XVI, Encyclical, *Verbum Domini* (2010). At www.vatican.va

according to serious historical method, and that other and hermeneutical approaches need to be carefully evaluated before being applied to the sacred text.

The upshot of these documents, as indeed of the writings of traditional Protestant thinkers too,[104] is the same. The Gospels must be studied according to the principles of genuine historical research, and a historical critical method with a focus on literary detective work and a concomitant dismissal of the extrinsic, historical evidence is not endorsed at all.

Research, however, that is not prejudicial or a priori but well founded in principles proper to history and to literary analysis is encouraged and embraced. The aim is less to settle specific questions (for instance about the precise order and relation of the Synoptic Gospels) as to settle how to go about settling them, namely scientifically and not arbitrarily.

Section 2: A Compelling Theory

Fine examples of such a sound approach to the Gospels and to their authenticity and authorship as based on historical and literary data had appeared before the last of the above documents was published. These examples gave full weight to the historical evidence about the Gospels, and nevertheless combined with this evidence a fine and subtle use of literary critical analysis in a diachronic way.

The path was marked out, in fact, by Protestant thinkers, notably Farmer, and was cleverly developed by a Catholic and an Anglican working together, Orchard and Riley.[105] Farmer pointed out in a multitude of ways that the literary phenomena of the Synoptic Gospels, which scholars had started trying to explain on the basis that Mark was first, could be as well and indeed better explained on the basis that Matthew was first and

---

[104] For example Farmer, *The Synoptic Problem*.

[105] Farmer, *The Synoptic Problem*, 199-232, Orchard and Riley, *The Order of the Synoptics*, 229-279. The same thesis has recently been further elaborated by Dennis Barton, *The Clementine Gospel Tradition*.

that Mark was dependent on Matthew and even on Luke. The particular details are too long to go into here.[106] What is of interest is how Riley and Orchard cleverly used Farmer's results, and their own, to show how, in full agreement with the historical evidence about dating and authorship, Mark could concretely have arisen out of Matthew and Luke.

The story is essentially simple. Matthew was first and was written for the purposes of the Church and the evangelizing mission of the Apostles at an early date, early enough indeed to be able to be quoted without need of named reference already by 50 AD in Paul's letters to the Thessalonians (as already noted above). That the Apostles would feel the need of a written record, either as aide-mémoire for oral teaching or also for the needs of converts in a literary culture (as Jewish culture was), and that Matthew, a tax collector practiced in keeping records and writing reports, should be chosen as scribe, make perfect sense.[107] It would also make perfect sense that no other written record, at least of an official or ecclesial nature, would be felt to be needed.

Such a need would however be felt as the Church became more universal with the inflow into it of Gentiles who had no Jewish background or culture. Matthew is distinctively Jewish in style and focus, and may indeed have first appeared in Hebrew,[108] which was not, to be sure, a problem (his Gospel was sufficiently full and accurate), but a Gospel that responded more directly to Gentile needs and expectations would

---

[106] The details are given in Farmer, *ibid.*, and Orchard and Riley, *ibid.*

[107] We are permitted indeed to conjecture that Matthew, as a professional record keeper well supplied with writing tools, began keeping notes of what Christ said and did as soon as he began to follow him.

[108] Orchard and Riley, *The Order of the Synoptics*, 198-199, doubt that Matthew was first written in Hebrew and think that Papias' remark that it was written 'in the Hebrew dialect' refers to style and not to language. They also think that it was a misunderstanding of what Papias meant that led to the view that Matthew was first written in Hebrew. But the belief in an initial Hebrew Matthew is so pervasive in the tradition that it is unlikely it could have arisen from a misreading of a single source. It is more likely to have arisen from several sources and, for this reason, more likely to be true. Incidentally, Kümmel *Introduction*, 44, rejects the view that Papias is referring to style and not language.

soon have seemed desirable. It would certainly have seemed desirable to St. Paul whose mission was to the Gentiles. That the Gospel of Luke was written by Paul's companion of that name is the unanimous view of the historical record, and that this Gospel, while not denying anything of the Jewish context of Jesus' life, nevertheless endeavors to make it all more intelligible to Gentile readers, is plain to view (as noted, Luke gives dates for the events of the Gospels according to Roman and not Jewish chronological facts).

Paul was naturally very anxious that his mission to the Gentiles should be acceptable to and agree with the complementary mission to the Jews and indeed with the rest of the Church in general, above all with Peter and other acknowledged leaders (as he makes plain in *Galatians* 2.1-10). Accordingly, Paul would also be anxious to have Peter's approval for Luke's Gospel. So since there is some evidence that Paul's desire to go to Rome had some special reason behind it (*Romans* 1.8-15, *Acts* 28), the conjecture is that Paul wanted to get Peter's approval for the Gospel already written by Luke, but not yet released.[109]

The form this approval took can be discerned from the Gospel of Mark, which tradition assures us is the record by Mark of Peter's preaching. As Orchard and Riley point out, and as was already in part anticipated by Farmer,[110] Mark seems to take the form of comments on sections of Matthew followed by comments on sections of Luke in a progressive manner that seems to reflect the steady and parallel unrolling in turn of the papyrus scrolls on which both Gospels would each have been written at the time. The result is that, as is evident from the texts themselves, Mark follows either Matthew or Luke but never both at the same time, never goes backward in either Gospel, and yet adds distinctive comments of its own to what the other Gospels say, often comments of a kind that an eyewitness would be likely to make. If Mark is a record of Peter's preach-

---

[109] The conjecture is not a mere conjecture but based on plausible inferences: Orchard and Riley, *The Order of the Synoptics*, 246-262.

[110] Farmer, *The Synoptic Problem*, 199-232; Orchard and Riley, *The Order of the Synoptics*, 262-277.

ing with Matthew and Luke before him in this fashion, then the literary features of Mark and their complex relationship to Matthew and Luke follow neatly and nicely into place.

The existence of Mark alongside Matthew and Luke would thus also neatly be explained. For there is little problem about why Matthew was necessary (the early Church needed it), or why Luke was necessary (the Gentile Church needed it), but there is a problem about the necessity of Mark, since Mark follows Matthew and Luke so closely and adds very little that is new. The answer is that Mark was necessary, or rather Peter's preaching as related to Matthew and Luke was necessary, in order to give to Luke the imprimatur of ecclesial approval which Paul needed. That Peter's preaching was recorded by Mark and then, unbeknownst at first to Peter, made available to Peter's initial hearers, confirms the somewhat "accidental" character of Mark. That Mark's record was nevertheless asked for by Peter's hearers and treasured by them is hardly surprising, because not only does it have Peter as source but it preserves what must have been his distinctive voice and memory of the Lord. Its asides and additions and even its abbreviations add a color and an energy that recall the vividness of the actual events.

Such at any rate in sum is the account given by Orchard and Riley of the origin of the Synoptic Gospels. What is striking about this account is how it treats the Gospels as genuinely historical records and accepts the historical evidence about the dating and authorship of them. Yet, without rejecting any of this historical evidence, it exploits all the techniques of the synchronic and diachronic method to uncover how the Gospels, and especially the Gospel of Mark, most likely came to be written.

This account illustrates everything that sound historical research could possibly want about any history of Jesus or any examination of the historical documents about Jesus. There is no need, and certainly no warrant, to go looking around for other and fancier theories of how Matthew and Luke followed Mark or Q or each other. All such theories are exploded, and in fact were long ago exploded, by the historical evidence about the Gospels.[111] There is no need to pay them further attention (save perhaps as here and there they may contain a literary insight). Rather there is need on scientific and historical grounds to reject them. The only theories worth paying attention to are those that accept and follow the historical evidence and that, as historical science requires, use the literary critical evidence in concert and harmony with the historical evidence to come up with an account of the origin and authorship of the Gospels that saves all this evidence, instead of saving some at the expense of others, or even of saving none but scholarly opinion. For assuredly the historical evidence is against all modern opinions that put Mark first, and the literary critical evidence, fairly considered, is against all such opinions too. Riley and Orchard and Farmer and others have firmly established that fact at least.

Now Riley's and Orchard's theory, however compelling and attractive it otherwise is, and however useful as an illustration of how to combine history and literary criticism in a wholesome and creative unity, is not perhaps the only one compatible with the historical and literary evidence. It may need qualification or addition or even replacement. Perhaps Mark is relative only to Matthew, and Luke is following Matthew and then finds Mark later.[112] All the Gospels, including John, or parts of them, may also have reached some sort of written or semi-canonical form very early on, for the material of the Gospels would have appeared very early on in the oral preaching of the Apostles (cf. *Acts* 4.19-20). Luke in the opening words of his Gospel (*Luke* 1.1-4) refers to many written and oral eyewitness sources that he knew of and had access to. Certainly Luke contains

---

[111] Cf. Camerlynck and Coppieters, *Synopsis Evangeliorum*, xxxi-xxxii: "omnia testimonia quae de ordine compositionis horum Evangeliorum agunt, Matthaeum primum scripsisse testantur... Si igitur aliqua dependentia mutua inter Mt. et Mc. sit admittenda, prioritas Mt non potest in dubium vocari..." "All the testimonies that deal with the order of composition of the Gospels give witness that Matthew wrote first... So if any dependence between Matthew and Mark is to be admitted, the priority of Matthew cannot be called into doubt." See also Orchard and Sutcliffe, *Catholic Commentary*, §§614d, 615a, p.764.

[112] See Chapman, John and John Barton, *Matthew, Mark and Luke: a study in the order and interrelation of the synoptic Gospels.* (London: Longmans, Green, 1937).

material not found in Matthew or Mark or even John (as the Emmaus resurrection story discussed above), and he must have obtained this material
from some of his original sources.

John is an even more striking case, since much of his material differs more from the other three Gospels than they differ from each other.
Orchard and Riley, given their focus on the Synoptic Gospels, say little
about John. Our historical sources, however, say a great deal, and certainly enough to explain very neatly its peculiar character.[113] First these
sources are unanimous in putting John's Gospel last but not so far distant
from the others that the other Apostles were no longer alive when it was
written. The Muratorian Canon says John wrote it at the insistence of his
fellow disciples and bishops, that the Apostle Andrew and other Apostles
were to tell John what came to the mind of each and that he was to write it
down in the name of them all. Since Andrew is alleged to have been martyred around 70AD, John's Gospel must be close to the date of Luke's and
Mark's. Clement of Alexandria also speaks of John composing a "spiritual" Gospel to complement the other three.[114] This remark both makes
clear that John wrote after, but in full awareness of, the other three, and
reflects the status of John as enjoying an especially intimate relationship
with Jesus. For such intimacy would have induced John to remember and
penetrate more deeply into the spiritual dimension of Jesus' discourses.

Clement's account is confirmed by the Old Latin Prologue to John,[115]
which also gives further reason for the distinctive character of that Gospel.
It says, first, that John wrote against the Ebionite heretics who were denying
the divinity of Christ (hence its opening "In the beginning was the Word").
Second it says that John decided to record the earlier parts of Jesus' public
ministry (before the imprisonment of John the Baptist), which the other
Gospels say little about. So while Jesus' public ministry seems to last about a
year in the other Gospels, it lasts closer to three years in the Gospel of John.

---

[113] Orchard and Riley, *Order of the Synoptics*, 139,

[114] Orchard and Sutcliffe, *Catholic Commentary*, 777a p.972

[115] Orchard and Riley, 151-155

These details about John's Gospel, which are preserved in historical records, give immediate and clear answers to the questions raised by John's Gospel. Of course, one may dismiss them as ex post facto stories devised precisely to answer those questions. But, first, such dismissal is itself a mere assertion and as easily dismissed itself as an ex post facto invention to support the theories of the historical critical method. Second, the stories contain certain incidental historical remarks (the Ebionite heresy, the Apostle Andrew, and other details[116]), which, being tangential to the stories insofar as the stories answer the questions, suggest there is real fact behind them. Third, the stories are much closer to the events than modern scholars are, and since the stories are plausible and believable enough, there is no reason to reject them, and certainly none to reject them so as to serve the purposes of the historical critical method.

But no matter, for whatever the details of the account one gives of the order and relationship of all four Gospels with each other, the fundamental facts of dating and authorship cannot be in doubt. The Gospels are the works of their named authors; they were all composed, in part or in whole, within decades of the events; among them Matthew is certainly first and John last (at least in final form). Some question arises about the order of Luke and Mark, but it seems clear they were relatively close in time and that they have some dependence on each other as well as on Matthew. Perhaps scholars will eventually be able to reach some final consensus on the nature and extent of this dependence. But what there can be no doubt about, once the historical evidence is acknowledged and fully weighed, and once the historical critical method has been fully and fairly judged, is that all four Gospels are the authentic writings of their traditional Apostolic authors. These writings accurately record the living memoirs of eyewitnesses, or eyewitnesses of eyewitnesses, about the real and historical Jesus, the same Jesus who was then and is now the object of Christian faith. No other judgment about the Gospels and their authors is rationally or historically defensible.

---

[116] As mentioned in the previous three notes.

CONCLUSION

TRADITION REVIVED

To highlight, then, as well as to contextualize these results, and to keep to the ecumenical character of the opinions and evidence at issue here, it may be worth ending with some quotations from the book *Jesus of Nazareth* by Cardinal Ratzinger (aka Pope Benedict XVI emeritus).[117] The Cardinal is a scholar in his own right, fully conversant with modern scholarship on Biblical questions. His opinions carry weight, and it will not be amiss to see how they tie in with the main claims of this book.

In the first volume of the cited work Ratzinger offers his own reflections on the historical critical method. The method he takes to be in essence necessary and positive. But it is clear that he does not think it justifies anything like Meier's distinction between history and faith, or between the historical and the revealed.

> The historical critical method – specifically because of the intrinsic nature of theology and faith – is and remains an indispensable dimension of exegetical work. For it is of the very essence of biblical faith to be about real historical events... The *factum historicum* is not an interchangeable cipher for biblical faith, but the

---

[117] Ratzinger, Joseph *Jesus of Nazareth. From the Baptism in Jordan to the Transfiguration.* Trans. Adrian J. Walker. (New York: Bloomsbury, 2007)

foundation on which it stands… [F]aith must expose itself to the historical method – indeed, faith itself demands this…[118]

Ratzinger admits that the historical critical method as such stays within the past and examines biblical texts as they are a datum from the past. But it thereby has to remain open to other facts, as the fact of the development of the unity of the Bible as in some sense a single book. It also has to remain open to the facts of what happened in the development of the Christian Church and of how the historical man Jesus could be behind it all. These facts may, strictly speaking, go beyond the focus of the historical critical method on this or that text or Gospel, and to this extent the historical critical method is limited. But if we take into account the larger historical context – the context of the Bible as a unity and the context of the Christian Church as a historical reality – the historical critical method itself allows us to discern something more, to discern indeed the historical Jesus as God Incarnate. Here Ratzinger, without using the explicit words, is entering upon the existential character of history, and showing how the Gospels are part of and speak to that existentiality. As he says further:

> I wanted to treat the Jesus of the Gospels as the real "historical" Jesus. I am convinced…that this figure is much more logical and, historically speaking, much more intelligible than the reconstructions we have been presented with in the last decades… Unless there had been something extraordinary in what happened, unless the person and the words of Jesus radically surpassed the hopes and expectations of the time, there is no way to explain why he was crucified or why he made such an impact… Isn't it more logical, even historically speaking, to assume that the greatness came at the beginning, and that the figure of Jesus really did

---

[118] Ratzinger, *Jesus of Nazareth*, xv-xvi.

explode all existing categories and could only be understood in the light of the mystery of God?"[119]

So much is compelling and something that this book too has sought to expound and defend. There is only one point on which I would demur. For Ratzinger then adds:

> Admittedly, to believe that, as man, he truly was God, and that he communicated his divinity veiled in parables, yet with increasing clarity, exceeds the scope of the historical method.[120]

Perhaps such belief does exceed the scope of the historical critical method, but it does not exceed the scope of history, or it does not exceed the scope of history seen in its grand sweep through the coming together of the Bible and the building up of the Church. Nor does it exceed history in the existentiality of the universal human condition. That the man Jesus is God is a historical fact, but a historical fact by way of necessary inference. The element of inference explains why the historical fact can be denied. To observe Jesus walking on the water is not inference but direct evidence. To say he did so by his own divine power is inference. The inference can be rejected. But some inference to a cause is required, and to deny the only sound inference, however possible it may be psychologically, is impossible historically. To say that the evidence belongs to history or to the historical method, but that the inference does not, is to take a limited view of history. No historian does or should refrain from inferences to causes on the alleged ground that the inference is not evidence but inference from the evidence. No general who won or lost a battle is or should be content to record the observed events and not try to discern the causes that explain them. Even less a military historian. Why

---

[119] Ratzinger, *Jesus of Nazareth*, xxii-xxiii.

[120] Ratzinger, *Jesus of Nazareth*, xxiii.

then should the Gospels and the historical method applied to them be any different?

The observable happenings which history records and with which it begins are never separable from the search for the causes: history is investigation, a search for the why; it is not mere chronicling. The Gospels are histories in this sense, and in this sense must they be read. A historical method that is truly critical, that truly *judges* what happens, can never be as limited as the historical critical method professes to be. The happenings about Jesus of Nazareth are not dealt with historically if they are merely recorded and not also investigated. Investigation, however, because of its existential dimension, takes us exactly where Ratzinger himself in fact goes:

> Isn't it more logical, even historically speaking, to assume that the greatness came at the beginning, and that the figure of Jesus really did explode all existing categories and could only be understood in the light of the mystery of God?[121]

Yes, indeed. And a true historical critical method would go there too.

---

[121] Ratzinger, *Jesus of Nazareth*, xxii-xxiii.

APPENDIX

HORNE ON EVIDENCE
FOR THE GOSPELS

There are ten lists for the catalogue or canon of the books. Of these, six agree exactly with our present canon, namely the lists of Athanasius (315AD), Epiphanius (370AD), Jerome (392AD), Rufinus (390AD), Augustine (394AD), and of the forty-four bishops assembled in the third council of Carthage (at which Augustine was present, 397AD). Of the other four catalogues, those of Cyril Bishop of Jerusalem (340AD), of the bishops at the synod of Laodicea (364AD), and of Gregory of Nazianzen, Bishop of Constantinople (375AD), are the same with our canon, excepting that Revelation is omitted; and Philaster or Philastrius, Bishop of Brixia or Brescia (380AD), in his list, omits the Epistle to the Hebrews and Revelation, though he acknowledges both these books in other parts of his works. [pp.71-72]

Horne then proceeds (pp. 72-85) to list Eusebius (ca. 260-340AD) and his account of the canon, Arnobius (ca. 300AD) and Lactantius his pupil, Novatus in Rome (ca. 251AD), Dionysius in Rome (ca. 259AD), Commodian (ca. 270AD), Anatolius at Laodicea (ca. 270AD), Theognotus (ca.282AD), Methodius in Lycia (ca. 290AD), Phineas of Thumuis in Egypt (ca. 296AD), Origen, Gregory of Caesarea and Dionysius of

Alexandria (pupils of Origen, ca.184-253AD), Cyprian of Carthage (d. 258AD), Caius Romanus (d. 296AD), Hippolytus Portuensis (ca. 160-235AD), Ammonius (who composed a harmony of the four Gospels, ca. 220AD), Julius Africanus (ca. 160-240AD), Tertullian (ca. 155-240AD), Clement of Alexandria (ca. 150-215AD), Theophilus of Antioch (ca. 181AD), Athenagoras (ca. 180AD), Irenaeus (ca. 140-202AD) disciple of Polycarp, himself a disciple of the Apostle John), the Muratorian Canon (ca. 170AD), Melito of Sardis (d. ca. 180AD), Hegesippus (ca. 100-180), Tatian (ca. 172AD), Justin Martyr (ca. 89-164), Papias of Hierapolis (ca. 110/116AD). He lists finally the Apostolic Fathers who, if they do not name in their surviving letters the books of the New Testament or the Gospels, contain evident references to them. They are Barnabas (martyred ca. 61AD), fellow laborer of Paul, Clement of Rome (90AD), Ignatius of Antioch (d. ca. 107/116AD), Polycarp (d. ca. 155AD). Finally he adds cross references within the New Testament itself, as Paul's quotation in *1 Timothy* 5.18 of a phrase of Jesus that occurs only in *Luke* 10.7, an implicit reference in *James* 2.8 to *Matthew* 22.39, Peter's explicit reference to the letters of Paul (*2 Peter* 3.16).

Horne, however, does not stop here with these names alone but refers also to certain heretical writers. It was the practice of such writers to wrest or erase particular passages of the New Testament that did not agree with their tenets, and they thereby gave evidence that the writings of the Apostles they altered were indeed writings of the Apostles, and writings, moreover, held in authority by the then existing Christian churches. Thus the words of Simon Magus, contemporary with the Apostles, as cited by Hippolytus Portuensis are coincident with words in Matthew and possibly with some in John. Cerinthus, contemporary with John, denied the letters of Paul but accepted the Gospel of Matthew (from Eusebius 6.9). The like holds of the Ophites, described by Hippolytus (*Against Heresies* 5.6), the Ebionites (Eusebius 3.27), the Basilidans and Valentinians, Marcion (ca. 85-160AD). In addition to such heretical authors, Horne mentions writings by opponents of Christianity as Celsus (ca. 170), Porphyry (ca. 234-305), the Emperor Julian (331-363AD), who cite the

Gospels and other New Testament writings as such, though of course in order to reject them.

This summary review of Horne's discussion (which could no doubt be found equivalently in other writers of the same or similar period) may seem to have been unduly prolonged. But it nevertheless has a certain utility for completing and confirming all the historical evidence for the authenticity and authorship of the Gospels (as of other writings in the New Testament). A final quotation, then, from Horne may serve as conclusion of the summary:

> The contents of the several books are precisely the same now as they were in the first two centuries; to which fact we may add that the multiplication of copies, which were read both in public and in private, the reverence of the Christians for these writings, the silence of their acutest enemies, who would most assuredly have charged them with the attempt [to alter them] if it had been made, and the agreement of all the manuscripts and versions extant, are all so many proofs of the integrity and incorruptness of the New Testament; which are further attested by the agreement with it of all the quotations from it which occur in the writings of Christians from the earliest age to the present times. [p. 451]

BIBLIOGRAPHY

Augustine, St., *De Consensu Evangelistarum*, or *The Harmony of the Gospels*. At http://www.ccel.org/ccel/schaff/npnf106.html

Barton, Dennis, *The Clementine Gospel Tradition*. Online at: http://www.churchinhistory.org/pages/book-clementine-tradition-edited-version/The-Clementine-Gospel-Tradition-by-Dennis-Barton-edited-version.pdf

Benedict XVI. *Verbum Domini*. 2010. At the Holy See, www.vatican.va

Brown, Raymond. *The Critical Meaning of the Bible* (London: Chapman, 1981).

Bultmann, Rudolph (and five critics), *Kerygma and Myth*, edited by Hans Werner Bartsch, trans. Reginald H. Fuller. Harper and Row: New York, 1961

Bultmann, Rudolph and Karl Jaspers, *Myth and Christianity. An Inquiry into the Possibility of Religion without Myth*, (New York: Noonday Press, Farrar, Strauss and Giroux, 1958).

Bultmann, Rudolph. *Existence and Faith: Short Writings of Rudolph Bultmann*, ed. and trans. Schubert M. Ogden (New York: World, 1966).

_____ *New Testament and Mythology and other Basic Writings*, ed. and trans. Schubert M. Ogden (Fortress Press, 1989).

Burridge, Richard A. *What Are the Gospels? A Comparison with Greco-Roman Biography.* Wm. B. Eerdmans Publishing: Grand Rapids, 2004

Camerlynck, A., and H. Coppieters. *Synopsis Evangeliorum.* Second Ed. Beyaert Publ: Bruges, 1910.

Egger, Wilhelm. *How to Read the New Testament: An Introduction to Linguistic and Historical-Critical Methodology.* Trans. Heinegg. Hendrickson: Peabody, Mass. 1996.

Eusebius Pamphilius of Caesarea, *Church History,* http://www. newadvent.org/fathers/2501.htm

Farmer, William R. ed., *New Synoptic Studies. The Cambridge Gospel Conference and Beyond.* Mercer University Press, Macon, GA. 1983.

Farmer, William R. *The Synoptic Problem. A Critical Analysis.* New York: Macmillan, 1964.

Fillion, L.C. *Life of Christ.* Herder: London, 1929.

Goldberg, Gary J. 'The Coincidences of the Emmaus Narrative of Luke and the Testimonium of Josephus,' *the Journal for the Study of the Pseudepigrapha* 13 (1995) pp. 59-77. This article can be found online at http://www.josephus.org/ GoldbergJosephusLuke1995.pdf. A shorter discussion to the same effect may be found at http://www.josephus.org/LUKECH. html.

Gorman, Michael J. *Elements of Biblical Exegesis: A Basic Guide for Students and Ministers.* Hendrickson: Peabody, Mass. 2010.

Hartlich, Christian. *Historical-Critical Method in its Application to Statements Concerning Events in the Holy Scriptures.* Trans. Darrell J. Doughty. At https://depts.drew.edu/jhc/hartlich.html

Herodotus, *Histories* 1.1, in *Herodoti Historiae*, Volume 1, Books I-IV, ed. Charles Hude (Oxford: Oxford Classical Texts, 1908).

Horne, Thomas. H. *A Summary of the Evidence for the Genuineness, Authenticity etc. of the Holy Scriptures.* Longman, Green, and Roberts: London, 1861.

Hume, David. *An Enquiry concerning Human Understanding.* Hackett: Indianapolis, 1993.

Josephus, *Antiquitatum Iudaicarum* ed. B. Niese (Berlin: Weidmann, 1892)

Justin Martyr, *S. Iustini Opera* ed. I.C.T. Otto (Jena: Mauke, 1847).

Kümmel, Werner G. *Introduction to the New Testament.* Trans. A.J. Mattill. SCM Press: London, 1966.

Lardner, Nathaniel. *The Credibility of the Gospel History; or, the facts occasionally mentioned in the New Testament; confirmed by passages of ancient authors who were contemporary with Our Saviour or His apostles, or lived near their time.* J. Chandler: London, 1727. Available online through books.google.com

Law, David. *The Historical Critical Method. A Guide for the Perplexed.* Continuum: New York, 2012.

Leo XIII. *Providentissimus Deus.* 1893. At www.vatican.va

Licona, Michael R. *Why are there Differences in the Gospels? What we can Learn from Ancient Biography.* Oxford: Oxford University Press, 2017.

Livy *Ab Urbe Condita, Praefatio,* in Titi Livii *Ab Urbe Condita* vol.1, eds. Robert Seymour Conway and Charles Flamstead Walters (Oxford: Oxford Classical Texts, 1914).

Lucretius *De Rerum Natura* IV.1090-1104, in *Titi Lucreti Cari, De Rerum Natura Libri Sex,* 2 vols., ed. Cyril Bailey, (Oxford: Oxford University Press, 1947).

Meir, John P. *A Marginal Jew. Rethinking the Historical Jesus.* 5 vols. Doubleday, and Yale University Press: London, 1991-2016.

Orchard, B. and H. Riley. *The Order of the Synoptics. Why Three Synoptic Gospels?* Mercer University Press: Macon, Ga., 1987.

Orchard, Bernard, Edmund Sutcliffe, et al. *A Catholic Commentary on Holy Scripture.* Thomas Nelson & Sons: London, 1953.

Paul VI. *Dei Verbum.* 1965. At www.vatican.va

Petersen, William J. 'Textual Evidence of Tatian's Dependence on Justin's Apomnemoneumata', *New Testament Studies* 36 (1990): 512-534.

Pius XII. *Divino Afflante Spiritu.* 1943. At the Holy See, www.vatican.va

Plato. *Republic*, 328c5-336a10 in *Platonis Opera*, Vol.IV, ed. John Burnet (Oxford: Oxford Classical Texts, 1902).

Plutarch, *Vitae Parallelae*, eds. Claus Lindskog and Konrat Ziegler (Leipzig: Teubner 1959-1980).

Pontifical Biblical Commission, *The Interpretation of the Bible in the Church.* 1994. At www.vatican.va

Ratzinger, Joseph, aka Pope Benedict XVI, *Jesus of Nazareth. From the Baptism in Jordan to the Transfiguration.* Trans. Adrian J. Walker. Bloomsbury: New York, 2007

Ricciotti, Giuseppe. *Life of Christ.* Bruce: Milwaukee, 1947.

Riddle, M.B. *A Harmony of the Four Gospels in Greek.* Revised ed. Houghton, Mifflin & co.: Boston, 1885.

Scotus, Bl. John Duns, *Opera omnia.* Vol. 1, ed. C. Balić, et al., Typis Polyglottis Vaticanis, Vatican City, 1950.

Simpson, Peter L. P. *Political Illiberalism.* Routledge, 1917

Simpson, Peter L. P. *The Great Ethics of Aristotle.* Routledge, 1917.

Socrates Scholasticus, *Church History* http://www.newadvent.org/fathers/26011.htm

Spinoza, Benedict, *Tractatus Theologico-Politicus,* 1670. Online at http://spinozaetnous.org/wiki/Tractatus_theologico-politicus

Tacitus, *Annalium Libri*, ed. C.D. Fisher (Oxford: Oxford Classical Texts, 1906).

Tacitus, *Historiarum Libri*, ed. C.D. Fisher (Oxford: Oxford Classical Texts, 1911).

Taylor, Vincent. *The Formation of the Gospel Tradition.* Macmillan: London, 1957.

Thucydides, *Historiae* 1.1-2, 22, in *Thucydidis Historiae*, ed. Henry Stuart Jones (Oxford: Oxford Classical Texts, 1942).

Warren, Mercy Otis, *History of the Rise, Progress and Termination of the American Revolution* (Boston: E. Larkin, 1805).

CPSIA information can be obtained
at www.ICGtesting.com
Printed in the USA
LVHW081131100419
613638LV00002B/7/P